A Yorkshire Year

CATHERINE WARR

First published in 2023
by Palatine Books,
Carnegie House,
Chatsworth Road
Lancaster LA1 4SL
www.palatinebooks.com

Copyright © Catherine Warr

All rights reserved
Unauthorised duplication contravenes existing laws

The right of Catherine Warr to be identified as the author of this work has been asserted in accordance with the Copyright, Designs and Patents act 1988

British Library Cataloguing-in-Publication data
A catalogue record for this book is available from the British Library

Every effort has been made to trace copyright holders.
Additional illustration by Penny Cameron.
Paperback isbn 13: 978-1-910837-44-3

Designed and typeset by Carnegie Book Production
www.carnegiebookproduction.com

Printed and bound by Micropress

Acknowledgements

I would like to thank my parents' collecting habits, because this book could not have been written if they, over the course of my life, had not obsessively bought any and all interesting, collectible, and antiquarian Yorkshire book they could get their hands on from charity shops and car boot sales. Our modest collection of over five hundred Yorkshire books enabled me to discover a vast range of information, a lot of which is difficult to find elsewhere.

I would also like to thank all the websites which made their information publicly accessible, especially Huddersfield Exposed and Project Gutenberg, whose collection of rare Yorkshire books in the public domain were crucial to my research. At a time when research materials are becoming increasingly locked behind paywalls, it is crucial that we enable as many people as possible to partake in historical research by making information easily accessible.

I would also like to thank the team at Carnegie, who took a chance on a young historian and her work.

Many thanks also to those who have provided photographs, particularly Averil Shepherd of Calendar Customs, whose website is an invaluable resource for the collection and study of British traditions, as well as the Knaresborough Lions Club, Goathland Plough Stots, and St Andrew's Dock Heritage Park Action Group. Thanks also to my parents for driving me to places so that I can source photos.

Introduction

A tradition is, as defined by the Oxford English dictionary, 'a belief, custom or way of doing something that has existed for a long time among a particular group of people'. It is a meaningful activity which has become significant among that community, and this book is intended to provide a comprehensive and immersive guide to the various customs, traditions, and folklore of Yorkshire, by taking the reader on a journey through the year.

Drawing on an extensive and varied range of sources – from historical to contemporary – this volume contains perhaps the largest single collection of Yorkshire folklore, customs, and traditions. This wide-ranging survey acknowledges that traditions are not immutable events in time; they are constantly changing and evolving, with some traditions dying out – later to be revived – and others being born. In recognition of this fact, this book includes a number of what could be described as contemporary customs, having originated within the last few decades, which have nevertheless proved to be meaningful practices within a community.

It is my hope that the reader is inspired by this collection to explore further the rich heritage of customs and traditions in our county, and so contribute to their persistence and revival.

A note on dates

For events or religious festivals which fall on different days each year, I have placed them on the date which they were last held; owing to the time of writing, this, except where noted otherwise, is 2019. These have been marked with an asterisk to denote that the date changes each year.

Because there are not 365 different events in the Yorkshire calendar, I have placed a variety of customs, folklore, traditions, songs, agricultural practices, and recipes in the remaining days to ensure a comprehensive and well-rounded collection. Though I have tried to maintain a balance in the distribution of these, there are certain months which contain more than others. This is due to the fact that those months have fewer events which take place; for example, many of the summer months are filled with fairs, festivals, and other events, and so do not contain as much of the aforementioned content as those with fewer events.

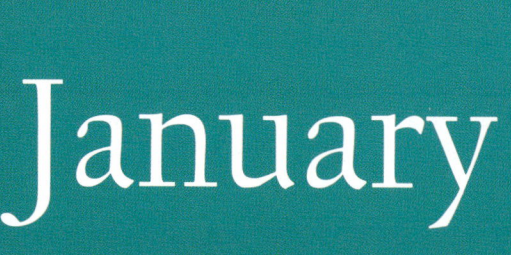

1st

As the first day of the new year, it was vital to ensure that you started off on the right foot. It was unlucky, for example, for fishermen to throw out ashes or sweep up dust on this day.

One major custom was that of 'first-footing', in which a 'Lucky Bird' (or 'Bod') was the first visitor to one's home. He must be a man with dark hair, and he must carry with him certain items to ensure good fortune for the rest of the year. These ranged from place to place but often included a piece of coal, bread, money, and a pinch of salt. These would be given to the house and exchanged for some food and drink.

Elsewhere, there was a much more elaborate ritual, as the food historian Peter Brears describes:

> At the annual meeting of the manorial court of Hutton Conyers near Ripon, the shepherds representing local townships came before the Lord of the Manor's steward and bailiff to obtain their grazing rights for the coming year. Each shepherd brought to court a large apple pie, about 16–18 inches in diameter, a twopenny sweetcake (except for one shepherd who provided ale instead), and a wooden spoon. Having measured and divided the pies with the aid of ruler and compasses, the bailiff proceeded to cut them in two, one half being shared between the steward, bailiff and tenant of the coney-warren, and the other divided among the six shepherds. The bailiff then gave each shepherd a slice of cheese and a penny roll and prepared the frumenty. [Frumenty is a type of porridge which was once very common in Yorkshire; a recipe can be found on 23rd January.] This was done by mixing it with mustard and placing it in an earthenware pot buried up to its rim in a hole dug in a field near the bailiff's house.

Driffield Penny Scrambling. Source: Averil Shepherd

The party then ate the frumenty, dipping in their wooden spoons in strict order of precedence, the steward being followed by the bailiff, the tenant, and then the shepherds. Refusing to take the frumenty was considered to be an act of disloyalty to the lord, so that any shepherd who forgot his spoon was forced to lie down and eat directly from the pot, some of his fellows always ensuring that his face was plunged into the glutinous yellow mass. Finally, the ale was served out, and the business of the court concluded in the bailiff's house.

One custom in Driffield is for children to scramble for pennies which have been thrown into the air. This would traditionally be accompanied by the rhyme ''Eere we are at oor town end, a shoulder o' mutton an' a croon ti spend.' Nowadays, though coin throwing is still practised, it is often replaced with sweets.

2nd

John Aubrey, in 1696, recorded one way of discovering the identity of your future lover. On the first new moon after New Year's Day, you must go outside and look up at the moon whilst saying:

> All hail to the moon, all hail to thee,
> I prithee good moon reveal to me,
> This night, who my husband must be.

You must then go to bed. Aubrey informs us that he personally knows two women who performed this ritual and later dreamed of their future husbands!

3rd

Famously told in William Wordsworth's poem of the same name, the White Doe of Rylstone is a legend of Bolton Abbey. As the story goes, a white doe was the companion of Emily Norton, a member of the Norton family who were involved in the Rising of the North. She would visit Bolton Abbey each week accompanied by the doe, and when she died the deer continued to make the trip by itself. However, as nice as the story is, there is no evidence to suggest that Emily Norton actually existed!

4th

'Riding the Stang' has been erroneously described as a New Year's Day custom, but there is little evidence to suggest that it was exclusively performed on that day. It was a form of community justice reserved for wife-beaters, and there were a number of rules to it. A witness of the custom practised in Guisborough in 1891 reported that:

Riding the Stang, from George Walker's 1814 *The Costume of Yorkshire*. Source: NYPL Digital Collections

The culprit's name must not be mentioned

The stang must be ridden in three separate parishes each night

The stang-master must knock at the door of the person they were holding up to ridicule and ask for fourpence.

An effigy of straw and old clothes was sat in an upright position on a cart along with the stang-master. The villagers, armed with pan lids, tin cans, and anything else which could make a noise, would then process to the front of the culprit's house where the stang-master would recite a rhyme. The crowd would then raise a 'tumult of sound, to which the wildest ravings of Bedlam would seem insignificant.' This would last for three nights, and at the end of the third night the effigy was burnt in front of the culprit's house.

5th

For many years in the late eighteenth century, the Unicorn Hotel in Ripon was famous for a man known as 'Old Boots'. Having entered the large pantheon of unusual and odd characters in Yorkshire folklore, here he is described in 1807:

> Among the infinite variety of human countenances, perhaps none ever so much excited astonishment and popularity as that of Old Boots, whose portrait has often been engraved. This extraordinary person was favoured by nature with a nose and chin so enormously long, and so lovingly tending to embrace each other, that he acquired by habit the power of holding a piece of money between them. Being a servant of the Unicorn Inn in Ripon, Yorkshire, it was his business to wait on travellers who arrived there, to assist them in taking off their boots. He usually introduced himself in the room with a pair of slippers in one hand and a boot-jack in the other, exactly in the attitude represented in his picture. The company in general were so diverted with his odd appearance that they would frequently give him a piece of money on condition that he held it between his nose and chin. This requisition he was always ready to comply with, it being no less satisfactory to himself than entertaining to them.

Many have claimed to see the ghost of Old Boots, who is said to haunt the hotel.

6th*

On Epiphany, in the village of Muker in Swaledale, it was customary to hold an 'Awd Roy'. Eight or ten lads would go about the village asking for food, wearing large aprons held out at the corners. Into these housewives would place cheesecakes – a type of curd tart, very different from what we would know as cheesecakes today – together with Yule loaves and other food to be eaten at a communal feast at the local inn. You can find a recipe for cheesecakes on 21st March, and Yule loaves on 11th December.

It is also traditional, on the first Monday of the new year, to hold a land auction at The George Inn at Hubberholme. The bidding – for sixteen acres of land just up the road – starts when a candle is lit and continues until the candle extinguishes itself. The proceeds raised from the auction go to the Poor Pasture Fund and is used to help locals in need. In addition, a candle is kept lit whenever the pub is open – a tradition originating, it is said, from the time when the pub was once the vicarage for the St Michael and All Angel's church nearby, and the vicar would keep a candle lit in the window to let parishioners know that he was available if needed.

7th

One legend claims that in the fifteenth century there lived at Barnburgh Hall, near Doncaster, a knight by the name of Sir Percival Cresacre. He was returning home one night on his horse when he was suddenly set upon by a huge wildcat. The horse bolted and threw Percival to the ground, where he was attacked by the cat. He managed to get away, albeit wounded severely, and staggered to St Peter's Church at Barnburgh. The cat followed him, however, and as he collapsed in the porch of the church he managed to crush the cat against the wall and kill it before dying himself. Inside the church you will find the effigy of a knight with a lion by his feet, a prop often used in dramatic retellings of the story.

8th

This song – 'The Old Woman in Yorkshire' – was first published in the early nineteenth century, but it is undoubtedly much older than that. It was very popular at the time and has since entered the repertoire of many Yorkshire folk singers.

There was an old woman in Yorkshire, in Yorkshire she did dwell;
She loved her husband dearly and another man twice as well.

Chorus
Ti me fal-the-doo-ra-lido, fal-the-doo-ra-lay

She went unto the doctor to see if she could find,
Something to give her husband for to make him blind.

She bought a stone of marrow bones and made him eat them all
The old man said, 'I am so blind I can't see nowt at all!'

The old man broken-hearted he unto her did say,
'I'm sure that I would drown meself if I could find the way!'

'If you will go and drown yourself, and that without delay,
If you will go and drown yourself, now I'll show you the way.'

So they both went hand in hand unto the river's brim,
The old man wadn't drown hisself unless she shoved him in.

So she stepped back a yard or two for to shove wiv all her might,
The old man quickly stepped aside and in she tummled quite.

Good lord how she did holler, good lord how she did bawl,
The old man said, 'I am so blind I can't see nowt at all.'

She swam until she floated unto the river's brim,
The old man took his walking stick and shoved her farther in.

So now me song is ended and what do you all think?
He's a damn poor singer if he didn't earn a drink.

JANUARY

9th

In the days before the NHS, when professional medical care was often unaffordable, many people relied on homemade cures – especially from certain women in the community who were regarded as 'wise women'. Hilda Jackson, from Bedale, tells the story in Dulcie Lewis' collection of Yorkshire cures of how her grandmother, born in 1855, was one such wise woman. The local doctor even recommended patients to her if he knew that they could not pay for their treatment themselves. 'Granny Myatt's Cough Cure' was one of her remedies, and consisted of 'half a pint of water, 1 teaspoon vinegar, 1 tablespoon golden syrup, 2 ounces butter, 1 pound brown sugar'. The ingredients would be put in a pan and boiled until all the sugar melted, and when tested in cold water it made a soft ball. These would then be sucked on until your tongue was sore, at which point the cough would be gone.

10th*

Plough Monday – the first Monday after Twelfth Night (see 11th January) – was the traditional start of the agricultural year, and after the Second World War efforts were made to extend the practices to the preceding Sunday. This has now become Plough Sunday, in which ploughs are blessed in churches and longsword dancing takes place.

The Goathland Plough Stots at the annual Plough Sunday service. Source: Goathland Plough Stots

The Fool's Plough, from George Walker's 1814 The Costume of Yorkshire. Source: NYPL Digital Collections

11th*

On Plough Monday it was customary for lads to beg throughout the village for money, which they would then either divide amongst themselves or put towards a communal feast – often against the threat of ploughing up gardens. It was also common to hold a mummer's play which George Walker, in 1814, describes:

> The principal characters in this farce are the conductors of the ploughs, the plough driver with a blown bladder at the end of a stick by way of whip, the fiddler, a huge clown in female attire, and the commander in chief, Captain Calf Tail, dressed out with a cockade and a genuine calf's tail, fantastically crossed with various coloured ribbons.

12th

If you encountered a woman who was a bit of a nuisance, one potential solution was to place her in the ducking stool. From the records of York Castle:

> Jan 12, 1657. Margery Watson, of Whitby, being a scold, to be ducked by the Constable, unless she within a month do ask Jas. Wilkinson and his wife, of Sneaton, forgiveness in Whitby church publiquely, and at the Cross in the market town there.

13th

George Hodgeson was born in Dentdale in 1621 and holds the honour of being the village's only alleged vampire. He died in 1715 and was buried in the churchyard, but soon began to be sighted in and around the village. Stories and rumours circulated – including a claim that he drank a glass of sheep's blood every day and could transform into a black hare – until, after a lengthy town meeting, it was decided that George should be exhumed and prevented from making appearances around the village. A brass stake was driven through his corpse and he was reburied, and no further sightings were reported. The top of the stake can still be seen poking through his gravestone.

14th

Near Giggleswick, by the side of the busy B6480, is the famous Ebbing and Flowing Well. This small well is able to drain and refill itself, and as a result of this unusual feature there is some folklore associated with it. It is said that a nymph, pursued by a satyr, was changed by the gods into the well, whose ebbing and flowing represents her sighs and tears. (For those curious as to why figures in Greek mythology are used in this tale, it is because it was common in the Middle Ages to use the term 'fairies' and 'nymphs' interchangeably, with 'satyr' often used to mean 'wild man'. The version of the story which I came across retained the use of Greek mythological figures).

15th

This song – 'The Wensleydale Lad' – was first published in 1892, but it is largely based on a much older song called 'Owd Ned's a Rare Strong Chap' which is set in Manchester. This version became immensely popular in the early twentieth century when it was printed en masse.

> Wey, what wi' me mother and father at 'ome I never 'ad any fun;
> They kept me gooin' from morn till night so I thought from them I'd roam.
> Now Leeds Owd Fair it were comin' on so I thought I'd take a spree,
> So I put me Sunday clothes on an' went whistlin' merrily.
>
> *Chorus:*
>
> With me bumpsy, bumpsy-ay, bumpsy, bumpsy annie,
> Bumpsy, bumpsy-ay and me bumpsy, bumpsy annie.
>
> Well, first thing I seen was a factory and I'd never seen one before;
> There were shuttles o' weave, shuttles o' tape they sell bi many's the score,
> And to every Ned there was a wheel and to every wheel a strap.
> I said ti t' master man, 'By gum, Owd Ned's a reight strong chap!'
>
> Well, then I went to Leeds Owd Church, never been to one in me days;
> Well I felt so ashamed o' missen 'cos I didn't know their ways.
> There were thirty, forty people in tubs so down wi' them I sat,
> When a saucy old bugger come up and said, 'Oi, kid, take off thi 'at!'
>
> Then in there come this great lord mayor an' ovver 'is shoulder a club,
> Well 'e got into a white sack-poke an' 'e got in the topmost tub;
> Then in there came this other owd chap, I think 'is name were Ned;
> Well 'e got into the bottommost tub an 'e mocked wor t' other chap's 'ead.

Now then there began this clatterin' row an' I couldn't make out what about,
Then the chap in the topmost tub he began a shoutin' out;
'E was tellin' us rich folks went to heaven while poor folks went to hell.
Well I thought to meself, 'Yer silly old bugger, yer don't know t' road yerself.'

Then they began to preach an' pray an' they preached for George ahr king,
Then the chap in the topmost tub 'e said, 'Good folks, let's sing.'
Well some o' them sang very well, the others did grunt an' groan;
Every bugger sang just what they would so I gave 'em Darby and Joan.

Then a chap came round wi' a box o' brass and 'e 'anded it all around;
Me not bein' a greedy sort I only took 'alf a crown.
Well a silly old bugger sat next to me I thought 'e were gonna dee.
I sez, 'Shurrup, thi silly old fool, there's plenty left for thee!'

When the preachin' an' prayin' was over and the folks were gannin' away,
I went to the chap in the topmost tub, said, 'Oi, kid, what's to pay?'
'Why, nowt,' says 'e, 'Me lad, tha must either be daft or fay!'
So I swung me clubstick over me shoulder, went whistlin' on me way.

16th*

The Goathland Plough Stots, a traditional longsword dancing group, perform their Plough Sunday dance on the first Saturday after Plough Sunday. Founded in 1922, the Goathland Plough Stots are one of the longest running longsword dancing groups in Yorkshire.

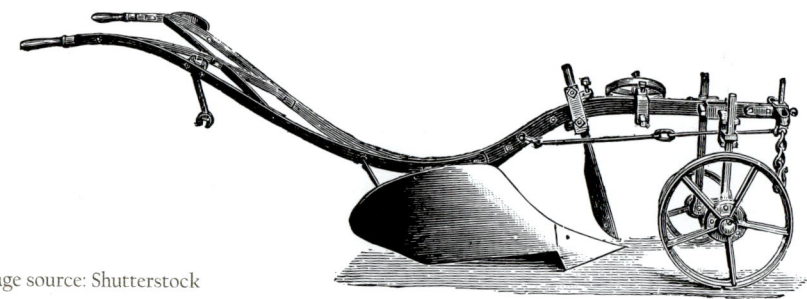

Image source: Shutterstock

17th

It was believed that if you drew blood from a witch, she could never harm you again. From this developed the story of an old man from Halifax who resolved to rid himself of a nuisance witch named Betty. Betty, it was believed, was able to change herself into a black cat. People were so scared of her that nobody dared to harm her, but the old man was not scared. Arming himself with a toasting fork, he set about trying to lure Betty in. He baked a cake and sat with it by the fire, and he was just on the point of nodding off when he suddenly saw a black cat sitting next to him. The cat did the usual cat things, but then, in a low, purring voice, said: 'Cake burns'.

'Turn it, then,' said the old man.

'Cake burns,' the cat said, louder.

'Turn it, then!' said the old man.

'Cake burns."

'Turn it, then!' roared the man. Instantly the cat gave a screech and flew up the chimney, and the old man made a wild stab at her with the fork. The cat vanished, but the man had succeeded in drawing blood. The next morning the witch was found in bed, with a wound on the same spot he had struck the cat. From then on, he was left in peace.

18th

The Peculiar (an old word meaning particular) Court of Masham was established by the Archbishop of York to deal with any offences in the area. This was done in order to reduce the amount of travelling between York and Masham. The chairman of the court was known as the Official and had a special seal, which is where the badge of Theakston's Old Peculiar beer comes from. The figure on the seal is believed to be that of Roger de Mowbray, who was Lord of the Manor and had been ransomed whilst a prisoner by the

Knights Templar during the Crusades. In gratitude, he donated funds from the church in Masham to the church of St Peter in York. The court consisted of 24 men (known as The Four and Twenty, which is the name of another Theakston beer), and held a considerable deal of local power. Some of the offences they dealt with include:

Not coming to church enough

Keeping a hat on at communion

Bidding the church wardens to do their worst on being asked to go to church

Not bringing their children to be baptised

Husband and wife living apart

Drunkenness

Swearing

Brawling and scolding

Harbouring Roman Catholic priests

Carrying a dead man's skull out of the churchyard and laying it under the head of a person to charm them to sleep.

The Peculiar Court of Masham badge, as seen on an Old Peculiar beermat. Source: Catherine Warr

19th

At the village of Laycock, near Keighley, lived a man named William Sharp who has since entered Yorkshire folklore as Three Laps. As the story goes, he fell madly in love with the barmaid of the Devonshire Inn at Keighley. They soon decided to marry. However, when Three Laps arrived at the church, his bride wasn't there – there had been an argument with the father-in-law over the marriage settlements, and so the wedding was off. This was more than Three Laps could bear. In 1807 he went to bed, and never rose from it again. For the next forty-nine years he stayed in his bed and refused to speak to anyone. He was thirty years old when he went to bed, and seventy-nine when he died on this day in 1856. His funeral at Keighley drew large crowds, and the coffin itself was a source of immense interest as, owing to his bed-bound life, his body could not be straightened out. The muscles of his knees and thighs had contracted, and so the coffin was significantly smaller and squarer than usual.

20th

There are many customs associated with this day – the eve of St Agnes – and one which took place in Yorkshire is that of the Dumb Cake. The rules of the ritual, as recorded in 1892, stated that four people had to make the cake in complete silence. When ready, it would be placed on a table in the middle of the room, and the four would stand in each corner. Every door of the house would be opened, and they would take an equal portion of the cake. The spirit of the future husband of one of the four would then appear, but only to the one destined to be his wife. Each girl would also take their portion of cake and walk backwards to bed, where they would eat it. If all the steps were followed correctly, it was believed that you would dream of your future husband. A variation on the ritual – performed on Midsummer Eve – can be found on 24th June. If you would like to try this custom yourself, then a recipe for Dumb Cake can be found on 30th January.

21st

Harpham is a small village in East Yorkshire. There are two stories associated with the well in the village, known as the Drumming Well. One is that, when William the Conqueror invaded the country, he promised the lands of Harpham to the first person to enter the village. The first was a small drummer boy, but a member of the St Quintin family was close behind and pushed the boy into the well in order to claim the land for himself. Hence, a ghostly drumming can be heard whenever a member of the St Quintin family is about to die. A more Quintin-friendly version is that, during an archery contest, a Quintin accidentally pushed a boy into the well where he died.

22nd

In Ripon, a horn is blown each night in continuance of a tradition which is over a thousand years old. Believed to have originated with the Ripon charter of 886, it began as a reassuring signal to the community that the watchman and his constables had taken over for the night. The horn is blown at each corner of the obelisk in the market square and then in front of the mayor's house.

Hornblowing at Ripon. Source: Averil Shepherd

23rd

Frumenty features a lot in the customs of this book, so if you would like to make it yourself, then here is a simple recipe. Though there are many variations, they all essentially contain:

- 1 pint of crushed wheat
- 1 pint of milk
- 1 pint of water

It is then cooked for three hours in a slow oven, sweetened with sugar, until thick and porridge-like. On very special occasions, it might be flavoured with spices, honey, or currants. Though perhaps not the most exciting of dishes, it was certainly a key element of traditional Yorkshire food.

24th

Across the River Esk at Glaisdale is a bridge known as the Lover's, or Beggar's, Bridge. The details of the legend associated with it change, but the general gist of the story is that Thomas Ferres was unable to cross the swollen river to say farewell to his beloved Agnes before leaving to fight the Spanish Armada in 1588. He promised that if he became rich, he would build a bridge across the river. This he did in 1619, and later became Lord Mayor of Hull.

25th

Wallops is a traditional Yorkshire game which resembles skittles. Nine wooden sticks are laid out in a square, and the object of the game is to throw sticks at them from a distance and knock down all nine in as few throws as possible.

The Lost Trawlermen's Memorial, Hull. Source: St. Andrew's Dock Heritage Park Action Group

26th*

Hull's vast maritime heritage brings with it the weight of many seafaring tragedies, and Lost Trawlermen's Day is an annual memorial service for the thousands of men who have lost their lives at sea. Held on the Sunday nearest to the 26th January, it particularly remembers the 40 men lost on the ships *Lorella* and *Roderigo* on this day in 1955.

27th

Though little remains nowadays, there was once a popular rag well at Walton, near Wakefield. Many Victorian writers refer to it as being a place where young lovers would tie scraps of cloth to the trees surrounding the well in the hope that the waters would grant them their wish. Though this seems to have declined by the early twentieth century, a visitor from 1935 recorded that, despite the well itself having vanished, people were still tying cloth to the trees – evidence that even when the object of a tradition vanishes, the power of belief it holds over people can still compel them to take part.

28th

Roger Dodsworth, in 1619, gave an account of a legendary creature known as the Slingsby Serpent:

> The tradition is that between Malton and this town there was some time a serpent, that lived upon prey of passengers, and which this Wyvill [a knight] and his dog did kill, when he received his death-wound.

At the local church of All Saints there is an effigy of a knight with a dog, believed to be that of a member of the Wyvill family who slew the legendary beast. However, stories about knights and dogs slaying dragons are very common in Yorkshire, as you will find out as you make your way through the rest of the book!

29th

Dulcie Lewis, in her collection of traditional Yorkshire cures, listed many home remedies for chilblains, a common ailment during winter. These include:

> Walking around the village barefoot in snow
>
> Standing in the snow to stimulate the circulation, then coming inside and rubbing the feet with a rough towel
>
> Rubbing the afflicted area with a piece of raw onion
>
> Soaking your feet in urine

Though they seem archaic and perhaps a little extreme to us today, many vouched for their effectiveness!

30th

The Dumb Cake, which was used for a ritual on St Agnes' Eve (20th January), is a rather plain cake by normal standards. The *Evening Telegraph*, in 1928, reported that it contained 'water, flour, sugar, and salt, and no other ingredient'! It is difficult to find precise recipes for the cake, but here are some instructions as found in a 1911 folklore collection from Peterborough.

Ingredients

- 1 spoonful of flour
- 1 spoonful of water
- pinch of salt

Method

- Mix the ingredients together and roll out

(There is unfortunately no guidance on how to actually bake the cake; however, I imagine a few experiments and a generous time at medium temperature should suffice).

31st

One old legend is that of the lost town of Semerwater. Though there are many variations of the story, they generally follow the same pattern. One day an old man, dressed in rags and leaning on a staff, came to the town and knocked on doors asking for food and water. One by one, each house turned him away, and as the day grew darker he eventually made his way to a small cottage on the side of a hill. The old man who lived there welcomed the traveller in and shared with him all that he had. When the traveller had rested, he went outside. There, in the twinkling of an eye, he changed; instead of an old man, he was now a young, handsome angel. He looked down at the town and cursed it. Then the sky darkened, the wind blew, and it rained all night long until the rivers flooded and the whole town was swept away – except for the little cottage on the hillside.

Semerwater as seen from Stake Road at Blean West Pasture. Source: Peter McDermott/Semer Water/CC BY-SA 2.0

February

1st

The term 'havercake lads' was a nickname given to soldiers of the 33rd Regiment of Foot, the Duke of Wellington's Regiment, after their unusual recruiting method. From the late eighteenth century onwards, recruiting sergeants would go around towns and villages in Yorkshire with an oatcake stuck on the end of a sword to entice men to join. Oatcakes were extremely popular in Yorkshire at the time, and you can find a recipe for them on 5th February.

A recruiting sergeant of the 33rd Regiment of Foot, from George Walker's 1814 *The Costume of Yorkshire*. Source: NYPL Digital Collections

2nd*

The feast of Candlemas – which celebrates the presentation of Jesus at the Temple – brought with it a superstition for the sailors of Yorkshire. 'A Candlemas crack' – a term for storms or heavy winds in February and March – 'lays many a sailor on his back'.

Since the 1990s, the Marsden Fire Festival has been held on the first Saturday in February every other year to celebrate the end of winter and the coming of spring. Inspired by the pagan festival of Imbolc (also known as St Brigid's Day), it features processions, dancing, costumes, fire, and spectacular pyrotechnics. It was held on this day in 2020.

The Marsden Fire Festival, or Imbolc. Source: Averil Shepherd

A Bishop Blaise procession, from George Walker's 1814 *The Costume of Yorkshire*. Source: NYPL Digital Collections

3rd

Today is the feast day of St Blaise, a fourth-century physician from modern-day Turkey. He was tortured with iron combs and executed for refusing to renounce Christianity. Because of the method of torture – combs were traditionally used on wool – he later became the patron saint of woolcombers. Unsurprisingly, there developed a particular fondness for him in areas where there was a large wool industry, especially in the West Riding. In Bradford, for example, there was a special festival held every seven years throughout the eighteenth and nineteenth centuries. Dr John Simpson, in 1825, records the scale and popularity of these celebrations:

> A herald came first ... Then a band of music. Afterwards the Woolstaplers on horseback riding on fleeces ornamented with sashes. Then the Spinners on horseback, with sashes and slivers of wool, blue coats and white stuff waistcoats; their horses covered with white worsted nets. Next ... the Masters' Sons and Apprentices on horseback most gaily dressed in scarlet stuff coats, white waistcoats, blue pantaloons, blue sashes and most beautiful caps ... Next came the Merchants on horseback ... [followed by] Jason and Medea [of the Golden Fleece myth] ... 'Bishop Blaise' passed followed by the Shepherd and Shepherdess ... Swains on horseback carrying crooks. Then came the Combmakers on horseback with combs and rams' heads with gilt horns ... Wool-sorters ... Master Dyers [...] The crowd in Bradford was immense for people came from all parts of the country and in all kinds of conveyances.

The popularity of St Blaise in Bradford continued further, with a middle school and streets named after him – and even a statue in the Wool Exchange!

4th

One rather dark folktale is that of the Penhill Giant. As the story goes, he was descended from the Norse god Thor and lived in a castle in Wensleydale with a herd of pigs and a Great Dane named Wolfhead. He would terrorise North Yorkshire, and one day whilst on a walk he saw a young girl with a flock of sheep. He set Wolfhead on them, and one by one the sheep were killed. The giant then began to assault the girl, but she managed to run away. Infuriated, he set Wolfhead on her, and the dog chased her across the ground. She hit it with a rock, but the giant, when he found her, swung at her with his club and killed her with one blow.

Sometime later, when counting his pigs, the giant noticed that one was missing. He angrily kicked Wolfhead, who was responsible for herding the swine. Wolfhead was ordered to search for the missing pig, and he soon found it – shot dead by a hunter. Furious, the giant ordered that every man in Wensleydale who could use a bow was to gather at a high cliff near Penhill – and anyone who refused would be killed.

At this point, Wolfhead had had enough. When his master called, he refused to come. Remembering how the giant had kicked him, he stayed in the forests. The giant angrily took a bow and arrow and shot dead the only friend he had.

Soon it was time for all the archers of Wensleydale to gather at the cliff. When the giant asked who had shot his pig, none answered because they did not know. Furious, the giant ordered that each man must bring with him his youngest son and await punishment. But then an old man, who was not afraid at all of the giant, said: 'Should you spill one drop of blood or cause one of the children to cry out in pain or fear, neither dead nor alive shall you enter your castle again.'

The next day, each man brought his youngest son to the hill. But they were surprised to find the old man there, and he said to each one: 'Fear not, your son shall return unharmed.'

The giant left his castle and was gleeful at the thought of how much pain and suffering he could cause. But he was met with a shock, because outside the castle – row after row – were his precious pigs lying dead. Each had an arrow in its body, and enraged, he vowed to slaughter everyone in Penhill. But then he saw the old man, holding a bow and smiling. The giant strode towards the old man, but suddenly froze and turned white, staring at something in the distance. There, behind the man, was the ghost of the girl he had murdered, holding the lead of Wolfhead. The dog strained at the lead, until the girl set him loose; he sprang and raced towards the giant, then leapt on him, and both went tumbling over the cliff.

5th

Oatcakes were extremely popular in Yorkshire and featured regularly in the diet of ordinary people. They would traditionally be made on a bakestone, but this recipe has been adapted for modern use.

Ingredients

- 170g oatmeal
- 90g plain flour
- 7g fast-acting yeast
- 1 tsp salt
- 250 ml milk
- 250 ml water

Method

- Mix together the flour, oatmeal and salt.
- Mix the milk and water and then warm in the microwave for around 40 seconds. Don't let it get hot!
- Mix the liquid with the dry ingredients and yeast to form a smooth batter. Set aside in a warm place for around half an hour.
- Cook in a well-greased frying pan until brown.

Image source: Shutterstock

6th

Knurr-and-Spell was once an immensely popular game in the North of England, especially Yorkshire, where it is believed to have originated. A long wooden bat – rather like a golf club – is the 'Spell' and is used to hit a small ball – the 'Knurr' – as far as possible. A springed 'trap' is often used to launch the Knurr into the air, where it is then hit by the player. Declining in popularity during the twentieth century, it was revived during the 1970s.

Knurr-and-Spell, from George Walker's 1814 *The Costume of Yorkshire*. Source: NYPL Digital Collections

The Devil's Arrows, Boroughbridge. Source: Catherine Warr

7th

The Devil's Arrows are three prehistoric standing stones in Boroughbridge which feature in a legend about the devil. As the story goes, he wanted to destroy the neighbouring town of Aldborough – though no particular reason is given as to why Aldborough was so deserving of the devil's wrath – and threw the standing stones at the town, but missed, hitting Boroughbridge instead.

FEBRUARY

8th

Pomfret cakes, or Pontefract cakes, are a special type of liquorice sweet which are famously made in Pontefract. There are records of liquorice being grown in the area from the seventeenth century, but it is likely that they were introduced to the town much earlier. Small and round, the cakes are stamped with a seal depicting Pontefract Castle, and the earliest recorded recipe for a similar type of sweet dates from 1678. By 1900, there were ten factories in Pontefract alone making liquorice, and in July each year a liquorice festival is held to celebrate its rich heritage in the town.

9th

There are a number of eyewitness accounts of ghosts which haunted Holy Trinity Church in Micklegate, York. The accounts reported three ghosts – two women and a child – which appeared on and moved across the East window. One was believed to be the mother, and the other the nursemaid. Other times, only one ghost was seen. However, in 1876, the Rector of the church wrote to the *York Herald* dismissing these sightings and explaining that it is simply due to people walking through the garden behind the window. He explained that, during a 12-month period when the ghosts were not seen, the vicarage house was empty. When a family moved in, the ghost sightings started again!

East Window, Holy Trinity. Source: Wikipedia Commons

10th

William Bradley, born on this day in Market Weighton in 1787, is one of the tallest British men ever recorded, standing at a height of 7ft 9in! He weighed a whopping 14lbs at birth and worked as a farmer before joining travelling freak shows as an attraction. He even visited George III, who gave him a large golden watch which he wore for the rest of his life. He died in 1820 aged 33 and was buried inside the church at Market Weighton. Giant Community Day – named in honour of the village's own resident giant – has been held every year between May and July since 1996, and features games, activities, and other family amusements.

William Bradley. Source: Wellcome Collection

FEBRUARY

11th

It is common, in folklore, for stories to take elements from other stories. This one, whilst clearly based on the story of Odysseus and Polyphemus, nevertheless has a Yorkshire flavour throughout. There once was a giant who lived in the village of Sessay, near Thirsk. He had 'the legs of an elephant, a visage terrifying to look upon, a single eye in the middle of its beetling forehead and a mouth as large as that of a lion'. He carried an entire tree as a cudgel, and would carry off whatever animals, food, or children he wanted and take them back to his cave. One day Sir Guy Dawnay – the son of Sir John Dawnay of Cowick Hall in East Yorkshire – encountered a beautiful young woman named Joan. He wanted to marry her immediately, and she agreed – but only if he killed the giant. One day, the giant strode up to a windmill to steal some grain. As he thrust a hand through a window one of the sails caught him on the head and knocked him unconscious. Seizing his sword, Sir Guy then ran up to him and stabbed the giant in the eye, killing him. There is another version, in which the giant kidnapped a boy named Jack and kept him as a servant. The giant lived at the mill, and ground men's bones to make his bread. Jack wanted desperately to escape and go to Topcliffe fair (see 18th July). One day, when the giant was asleep, Jack stole his knife and stabbed him in the eye. He then took the giant's dog, killed it, and wrapped the dog's skin around him, barking as he ran through the giant's legs to escape.

Image source: Shutterstock

12th

'The Terrible Knitters of Dent' were famed for their speed at knitting, quality of work, and the fact that they would knit non-stop. So well-known was Dent for its knitting that it was the location of knitting schools and produced more knitted supplies than anywhere else in Northern England. 'The True Story of the Terrible Knitters e' Dent', published in 1834 by Robert Southey, tells the story of two sisters who were sent to learn knitting in Dent and hated it. Knitting was non-stop, dawn until dusk, and if you didn't knit enough, you didn't get any supper. That – and the terrible food – caused the sisters to run away and tell their story to Robert many years later. Before they ran away, they had become so fast at knitting that they could knit an entire stocking in six hours.

Wensleydale knitters, 1814, from George Walker's *The Costume of Yorkshire*. Source: NYPL Digital Collections

13th

'In my childhood in the 1930s,' recalled Mac Webster from Sheffield, 'for a boil on the back of the neck you found a fresh cow pat, put it in some gauze and placed it on the boil to "draw" it.'

A cow and some boil poultice. Source: Shutterstock

14th

Rev. M. C. F. Morris, writing in 1892, recorded one unusual Yorkshire way of finding out the identity of your future lover. You might like to try this for Valentine's Day – all you need is a Bible and a key!

> In these cases the Bible would be opened at Ruth i. 16, 17, and the key placed in it there, and either fixed by a piece of string and the Bible suspended by another piece of string, or the key was simply placed in it at the chapter named and then set upon the table. The name of the wished-for husband was then mentioned, and if the wish was destined for fulfilment, the key in either case would be found turning towards the said verses.

15th*

The day before Shrove Tuesday was once known as Collop Monday, as it was customary to eat collops – slices of bacon or ham – with eggs. This was done in order to use up the last of the fresh meat before Lent.

16th*

On Shrove Tuesday, church bells would ring to signal housewives to start making pancakes and for apprentices and schoolchildren to leave their work for the rest of the day. This was also a time for 'barring-out', in which schoolboys would send their teacher outside and then bar the door, allowing him to re-enter only if he promised them a holiday.

In Scarborough, hundreds of people turn out to skip by the seaside. Originating in the early twentieth century, it replaced an earlier practice of playing ball games. In 1903 there was just a handful of children skipping; by 1927 it was a huge event involving hundreds of people. Fishermen would twine ropes together to stretch from one side of the road to the other, allowing as many as thirty people to skip at one time. The signal to start skipping is the ringing of the Pancake Bell, for one minute at noon, on a ship's bell hung in the Rotunda Museum.

William Henderson, writing in 1879, recorded that:

> I learn from a clergyman, formerly a scholar at the grammar-school of Sedbergh, in Yorkshire, that the master used to be entitled to 4d yearly from every boy on Shrove Tuesday to buy a fighting-cock.

FEBRUARY

17th*

Due to a mistaken association of 'ash' with 'hash', mutton hash was often eaten on Ash Wednesday. Sometimes 'fruttaces' or fritters were eaten, containing flour, eggs, apples, dried fruit, and spices. This custom is curious, as Ash Wednesday is the first day of Lent, and so all the fancy food was supposed to have been eaten *before* Ash Wednesday! You can find a recipe for fritters on 26th February.

18th*

The first Thursday in Lent was sometimes called Bloody Thursday, as it was customary in some parts (especially Cleveland) to eat black puddings.

19th*

Two days after Ash Wednesday was Kissing Friday, in which boys were allowed to chase and kiss girls without fear of rejection or punishment from parents. Though unthinkable nowadays, it was very popular even up to the 1930s. Boys would chase girls round the schoolyard, and some were even kept behind after school for an hour to delay their approach! This playground game may have originated from the story in the Gospels of Judas betraying Jesus with a kiss, prior to his crucifixion on Good Friday.

Facing page: the ringing of the Pancake Bell signals the start of the seaside skipping at Scarborough. Source: Averil Shepherd

20th*

For over 30 years the Slaithwaite Moonraking festival has been lighting up a dark night in February with homemade lanterns. Held every two years, the festival celebrates storytelling, particularly the tale of a band of smugglers who, when set upon by officials mid-smuggle, cleverly outwitted them by saying that they were 'raking the moon' – the reflection on the water! The festival creatively re-enacts this and other stories with crafted lanterns and costumes. It was held on this day in 2021.

Fantastic lights and home-made lanterns as part of the Slaithwaite Moonraking Festival. Source: Averil Shepherd

21st

The village of Austwick, in Craven, developed a reputation for having a lot of very simple folk, and so a number of stories emerged which poked fun at the inhabitants. Known as the 'Austwick Carles', the next four days exhibit some of the stories created about them. As one story goes, once upon a time the villagers only had one knife in the whole village. They kept it between two branches of a tree, but one day it was lost. After much searching it was finally found, but, with no suitable rock or tree on the moors where they could place it, they were stumped as to where to keep it. Then, one of them noticed the shadows that a cloud cast on the ground. They decided to put it there, so the shadow could tell them where it was. Unfortunately, when the cloud moved away and they followed the shadow, they could no longer find the knife.

22nd

Another story about the Austwick Carles claimed that Austwick Hall was a low building with a thatched roof. For many years the thatch had been neglected, and it began to grow moss and mould. One day, one bright spark suggested that, after observing a cow eating grass in a field, they lift up a cow to the roof so it could nibble off the unwanted growth.

23rd

On another occasion, an Austwick farmer was leading his bull out of a field. The field was enclosed by stone walls and only had a single gate. The farmer was stumped as to how to get the bull out. For several hours, as the story goes, he and his labourers tried to lift the bull over the gate. But they couldn't manage it, and so they called for help at a neighbouring village. A kind neighbour then opened the gate for them, and the bull went out.

24th

Our final story about the Austwick Carles claims that they knew that good weather was announced in the spring by the coming of a cuckoo. Noticing that good weather was there when the cuckoo was there, they decided to build a wall around the cuckoo to keep it there permanently, and so have good weather all year round. Unfortunately, it flew away, and so they had to wait until next year for it to return.

Cuckoo. Source: Pearson Scott Foresman

25th

One common folklore creature which can be found in Yorkshire is a hob, or hobman. A hob is, as a rule, 'an ugly shaggy little fellow without any clothes, but in spite of his appearance he is a hard worker and always friendly if not angered'. The surest way to vex him is to offer him clothes, especially costly or beautiful garments, hence the Yorkshire rhyme:

Gin hob mun ha'e nowt but a hardin hamp [a farm labourer's smock],

He'll come nae mair nowther to berr [to thrash] or stamp.

The most famous hob is the hob of Farndale. As the story goes, there once lived a rich farmer named Jonathan Gray. He was aided in his work by a hob, who had been with the farm since the days of Jonathan's grandfather. It was believed that the hob came to the farm after a servant called Ralph, who was one of the best labourers on the farm, froze to death on the moors. At night the family heard noises in the barn, and upon investigation found that more corn had been threshed in that single night than a man could do in a week. Hence, it was believed that the hob – or, as some believed, the spirit of Ralph – came to the farm and assisted with the work. Each evening a jug of cream was left in the barn as a present to the hob. Many years later, when Jonathan came to inherit the farm, his first wife died and he remarried. His second wife was much more miserly than his first, and was reluctant to leave a good jug of cream out each night. One night she swapped the cream for milk, and from then on the hob stopped doing any work. Even worse, the hob turned mischievous. Jonathan became dogged with bad luck, and everything that could go wrong at the farm did. Strange noises haunted the house at night, things went missing, and before long, none of the farm hands wanted to stay anymore. Jonathan and his wife decided to move, and when they had packed up everything, a neighbour called out to him and asked him what he was doing.

'We're flitting,' said Jonathan.

'Aye, we're flitting!' came another, unexpected voice. Jonathan turned round, only to find the hob sitting among his things! And with that, Jonathan turned round and headed home again.

26th

It was customary to eat 'fruttaces', or fritters, on Ash Wednesday. These taste rather like a rich fruit scone, and this recipe dates from the 1930s.

Ingredients

- 225g self-raising flour
- 85g white sugar
- 55g butter
- 28g candied peel
- 1 egg
- 55g currants
- ¼ teaspoon of salt
- A little milk

Method

- Mix the flour and salt and rub in the butter
- Add the sugar, currants and chopped candied peel
- Mix to a stiff dough with the beaten egg and a little milk
- Roll out on a floured board and cut into round discs
- Fry in butter for a couple of minutes each side.

27th

The Strid is an infamous stretch of the River Wharf, a deceptively perilous area which has sadly claimed many lives. Many legends have arisen about it, including The Boy of Egremont. As the story goes, he was the son of William FitzDuncan, a nephew of King David of Scotland. Born at Egremont Castle in Cumberland, in 1251 he went hunting in Wharfedale when he came to the river. Thinking the Strid easy to cross, he tried to leap to the other side but fell into the water. Caught by the hidden rocks and currents, he drowned. This legend has often featured a different person, and so it is difficult to establish whether it is based on a real event.

28th

The following account of an encounter with a barghest – a monstrous black dog common in Northern folklore – was published in the *Leeds Mercury Supplement* on 28th February, 1881:

> Of this mysterious personage (barghest) I am able to give a very particular account, having, only a few days ago, seen Billy B-y, who had a full view of it.
>
> 'You see, sir,' said Billy, 'as how I'd been a-clock-dressing at Gerston (Grassington), an' I'd stayed raither lat, an' may-be gitten a lile sup o' spirit, but I war far from bein' drunk, an' knaw'd everything 't pass'd. It war about eleven o'clock when I left, an' war at back end o' t'year; an' it war a grand neet. T' mooin war varra breet, an' I nivver seed Rylston Fell plainer in a' my life. Now, yo' see, sir, I war passin' down t' mill loin, an' I heard summat cum past me, brush, brush, brush, wi' chains rattlin' a' t' while; but I seed not; an' thowt I to mysen, now, this is a most mortal queer thing. An' I then stuid still, an' luik'd about me, but I seed nowt at a', nobbut t'two stane walls on each

side o't'mill loin. Then I heerd again this brush, brush, brush wi' t' chains; for, yo' see, when I stuid still it stopp'd; an' then, thowt I, thus mun be a Bargest, 'at sae mitch is said about; an' I hurried on toward t'wood brig, for they say as how this Bargest cannot cross a watter; bu, lord, sire, when I gat ow'r t'brig, I heerd this same thing again; so it wud oither hev cross'd t' watter, or gane round by t' spring head (only thirty miles!). An' then I becom' a valiant man, for I war a bit freeten'ed afore; an' thinks I, I'll turn an' hev a peep at this thing. So I went up greet bank towards Linton, an' heerd this brush, brush, brush we' t'chains a't'way, but I seed nowt; then it stopp'd a' of a sudden. So I turn'd back to gan hame, but I'd hardly reich'd t'door when I heerd again this brush, brush, brush, an' t' chains. Going down towards t' Holin House, an' I follow'd it, an' t' mooin then shone varra breet, an' I seed it tail! Then, thowt I, thou owd thing! I can say I've seen the' now, so I'll away hame. When I gat to t'door there wor a girt thing like a sheep, but it war bigger, liggin' across t' threshold o't'door, an' it war woolly like; an' says I. 'Git up', an' it wouldn't git up; then, says I, 'Stir thsel'!' an' it wouldn't stir itsel'. An' I grew valiant, an'rais'd t' stick to baste it up, an' then it luiked at me, an' sich oies (eyes)! They did glower! An' war as big as saucers, an' like a cruell'd ball; first there war a red ring, then a blue one, then a white one; an' these rings grew less an' less, till they cum to a dot! Now, I war nane fear'd on it, tho' it grinned at me fearfully; an' I kept on sayin', 'Git up an' stir thesel';' an' t'wife heeard as how I were at t'door, an' she cum to oppen it, an' then this thing gat up an' walk'd off, for it war more fear'd o' t' wife than it war o' me! An' I call'd wife, an' she said it war t' Barghest, but ah've nivver seed it since; an that's a true story.

29th

It was commonly believed that crops and plants sowed on a Leap Year day would grow back-to-front. This did not impress Charles Darwin, who wrote in his autobiography:

In illustration, I will give the oddest case which I have known. A gentleman (who, as I afterwards heard, was a good local botanist) wrote to me from the Eastern counties that the seeds or beans of the common field-bean had this year everywhere grown on the wrong side of the pod. I wrote back, asking for further information, as I did not understand what was meant; but I did not receive any answer for a long time. I then saw in two newspapers, one published in Kent and the other in Yorkshire, paragraphs stating that it was a most remarkable fact that 'the beans this year had all grown on the wrong side'. So I thought that there must be some foundation for so general a statement. Accordingly, I went to my gardener, an old Kentish man, and asked him whether he had heard anything about it; and he answered, 'Oh, no, Sir, it must be a mistake, for the beans grow on the wrong side only on Leap-year, and this is not Leap-year.' I then asked him how they grew on common years and how on leap-years, but soon found out that he knew absolutely nothing of how they grew at any time; but he stuck to his belief.

1st

Rev. M. C. F. Morris, writing in 1892, recorded a custom performed in Yorkshire which had declined by the time of writing. It was to ring a bell – known as the 'compline bell' – at six o'clock every morning and evening during Lent. Presumably originating as a means of calling locals to prayer, the practice seemingly lost its original purpose and survived only as a ringing of the bell.

2nd

The Harrogate sulphur waters have been attracting visitors for over four hundred years. First discovered in 1596, Edmund Deane, a seventeenth-century doctor, described them as being able to 'cheereth and reviveth the spirits, strengtheneth the stomache, causeth good and quick appetite and furthereth digestion'. The town boomed and became the trendy health spa for the middle and upper classes, gaining the reputation, according to Georgian doctor Thomas Short, of being 'the Rendezvous of wantoness and not seldom of mad Frolicks'.

One of the many wells in Harrogate from which visitors could draw the healing waters. Source: Wellcome Collection

3rd

This song, called the 'Pony Driver's Song', was collected from a coal miner at the Wheldale Colliery in Castleford. Operating for 117 years, it closed in 1987. Pony drivers were in charge of horses which pulled tubs of coal through the mine.

> Ah shall be glad when this shift is done;
> Ah shall be up there out in the sun,
> Tha'll still be down here in this dark 'oil,
> a grunting and groaning and pulling the coil.

Chorus

> For I am a driver, these are me tubs,
> Ah'm up the road, old boys, and my pony rubs,
> Where is the doggie? Nobody knows.
> He's dahn by the pass-by a picking his nose!
>
> All t' corn's in t' manger and watter's in t' trough,
> tha'll pull thi noase aht when tha's enough,
> Ah'll tek thee in t' standing and drop off thi gear.
> When Ah comes back Ah know tha'll be here.

4th

Christopher Pivett was an unusual character who has since entered the pantheon of odd people in Yorkshire folklore. When his house in York was accidentally burnt down, he resolved to never again sleep in a bed, in case he burned to death whilst sleeping or would not have enough time to escape with his property if another accident occurred. This he kept for the next forty years of his life, insisting on sleeping on the floor, on two chairs, or upright in a chair – but always dressed, presumably to allow for a quick escape from a fire. A reclusive figure, he seldom allowed anyone to enter his house, nor told anyone about his family or where he was born. He died in York in 1796 at the age of 93, and was buried with a human skull which he had kept in his house and strictly ordered to be buried with him.

5th

Diphtheria was a major killer before it was almost eradicated in the UK by a large vaccination program. One man, who was born in 1922 before the vaccine was available, recalled being made to stand 'over a fire shovel of red-hot coals, which was sprinkled with yellow sulphur powder' in the belief that this would prevent infection.

6th

In the village of Thrybergh, near Rotherham, stands St Leonard's Cross. One legend associated with it – first written down in the seventeenth century by Sir John Reresby – claims that Leonard de Reresby, his ancestor, was fighting in the Crusades when he was captured and held prisoner for seven years. His wife, believing him to be dead, was about to marry another man but, through the miraculous power of God, Leonard was transported to the church, still in shackles and chains. He arrived just in time to stop the marriage, but died shortly after. St Leonard's Cross is said to mark the place where he was buried.

7th

William Henderson, writing in 1879, recorded that it was customary in Yorkshire to pour boiling water over the doorstep after a bride had left home to marry; it was believed that before the water dried up, another marriage would be agreed on.

8th

Sir John Reresby – who wrote of St Leonard's Cross on 6th March – also wrote of a case concerning witchcraft which caused a stir at the York Assizes in March, 1687:

> An old woman was condemned for a witch. Those who were more credulous, in points of this nature than myself, conceived the evidence to be very strong against her. The boy she was said to have bewitched fell down on a sudden before all the court when he saw her, and would then as suddenly return to himself again, and very distinctly relate the several injuries she had done him. But in all this it was observed the boy was free from any distortion, that he did not foam at the mouth, and that his fits did not leave him gradually, but all at once; so that, upon the whole, the judge thought it proper to reprieve her. In which he seemed to act the part of a wise man. But though such is my own private opinion, I cannot help continuing my story. One of my soldiers being upon guard, about eleven in the night, at the gate of Clifford Tower, the very night after the witch was arraigned, he heard a great noise at the Castle, and going to the porch he there saw a scroll of paper creep from under the door, which, as he imagined by the moonshine, turned first into the shape of a monkey, and thence assumed the form of a turkey-cock, which passed to and fro by him. Surprised at this, he went to the prison and called the under-keeper, who came and saw the scroll dance up and down, and creep under the door, where there was scarce an opening of the thickness of half-a-crown. This extraordinary story I had from the mouth of both the one and the other, and now leave it to be believed or disbelieved, as the reader may be inclined, this way or that.

9th

It was compulsory, in seventeenth-century England, to bury people in wool. This was done in order to protect the English wool industry, which was often under threat from cheaper imports. In 1692 in Grinton, North Yorkshire, a man was fined £5 for burying his daughter in linen. The acts which enforced this were repealed in 1814.

10th

In Arthur Mee's tour of North Yorkshire, written in the early 1940s, he records that in the village of Faceby, in Hambleton, a woman was baking charity loaves in her cottage which were to be given each week to six poor folk. This was requested in Anthony Lazenby's will of 1634, and had been carried out faithfully for over 300 years.

Image source: Shutterstock

11th

If you have spent time in or around Bradford, you may have noticed a boar's head on the crest of the city. But why is it there? Well, as the story goes, a terrible boar was terrorising the area around Cliffe Wood. A reward was offered for anyone who could kill it, and so one huntsman tracked it down, killed it, and cut out its tongue to bring as proof. However, someone else found the boar and, cutting off its head, brought it to Bradford to prove that *he* had killed it. He was, however, discredited due to the missing tongue. The first huntsman received the reward, and the tongue-less boar remains on the city's crest to this day.

The Bradford Boar, as seen on the city's crest. Source: Catherine Warr

Whitby Abbey. Source: Catherine Warr

12th

Though difficult to establish the veracity of this legend, one story about Whitby Abbey holds that during the Reformation – when the abbey was dissolved and its riches plundered – a ship belonging to the King was taking its bells away when it suddenly sank. The legend holds that it is still possible to hear the bells under the water.

13th

Valley Parade, the home of Bradford City Football Club, sits on the site of a once-popular healing well. Known as Holy Ash Well, many would come to drink the waters on Sundays and other holy days. Close by it was a stone which was believed to cure warts. Pins, coins, rags and food were regularly left at the well as offerings. Eventually the well was built over and it now lies underneath the football stadium.

14th

The fourth Sunday in Lent was known as Carling Sunday. Carlings were dried peas which, after having been soaked in water overnight, were boiled and then fried in butter or lard. Such was the popularity of this food that, even in the 1860s, two to three hundredweight of carlings were sold each year in some small towns. The effect of carlings on digestion gave rise to the popular saying 'Carling Sunday, farting Monday'.

15th

One folktale is that of the devil and Filey Brigg. One day, the devil was building Filey Brigg when he dropped his hammer into the sea. Reaching into the sea to grab it, he picked up a haddock instead – which is why haddocks have two dark spots near their head, as these are the fingerprints of the devil.

Image source: Shutterstock

16th

One unusual and mysterious feature which can be found on houses and buildings in Calderdale are carved stone heads. Initially believed to be Celtic, they are now regarded as dating from the seventeenth to the nineteenth centuries. They can be found on doors, windows, bridges, gables, gateways, chimneys – all places related to entering and leaving – which has given rise to a theory that they were believed to help ward off evil spirits. As one, perhaps apocryphal, story shows, as late as 1971 the landlord of the Old Sun Inn in Haworth was advised by one of his regulars to place a carved stone head above the doorway to dissuade a ghost which was supposedly haunting the area. Over 600 of these heads have been found in Calderdale.

17th

S. Baring-Gould, whilst a vicar in Horbury, near Wakefield, wrote down this song which was sung to him by mill girls in 1864, titled 'The Heckler Lad'.

> I am a jovial heckler boy
> And by my trade I go;
> I trudge the world all over
> And get my living so.
>
> I trudged this world all over,
> A pretty maid I spied;
> I asked her if she would go with me
> And be my lawful bride.
>
> The pretty fair maid denied me,
> And said, 'If I do so,
> I shall be ruined for ever a day
> And shall be loved no mo.'

'Oh how will you be ruined?'
The heckler boy replied,
'For I am sure I will marry you
As soon as work I find.'

'Now hold your tongue from clattering
And tell me none of your tales,
For you are a jovial heckler boy
And that's your only trade.'

'How do you know me so, my dear,
And how do you know my trade?'
'I know you by t' fringes of your apron,
Of your apron,' she said.

'The fringes of your apron
And by your slender shoe;
Your stockings they are as white as snow,
So that's how I know you.'

I could not help for smiling
To hear the girl say so;
I threw my arm around her waist
And along we both did go.

She brought a glass all in her hand
And filled it to the brim;
'Here's to the health of each heckler boy
That calls my true love his.'

18th*

The oldest annual horse race in England is held every year on the third Thursday in March. Called the Kiplingcotes Derby, it was first held in 1519 and is unusual in that the runner-up often receives more prize money than the actual winner – first-place receives £50, whilst second-place wins a cut from every entry fee, often resulting in a larger sum. It is run on tracks and roads instead of a traditional racecourse, and so seriously is the tradition taken – the rules state that if the race is not run one year, it must never be run again – that on occasions when it has been necessary to cancel the race, locals take it upon themselves to walk a horse around the course to ensure its survival.

A rider in the Kiplingcotes Derby. Source: Averil Shepherd

19th

R. Bray, of Cleckheaton, swore by this method of curing warts: 'Put a piece of raw beef on top of the wart. Wish it away, then hide the piece of beef and do not tell a soul where you have hidden it. The wart will go away eventually – mine did in 1947.'

20th

One of the oldest Augustinian priories in England, Guisborough Priory was founded in 1119. It soon amassed huge wealth, and unsurprisingly there emerged a legend that a secret tunnel led from the priory to a cave in which a raven stood guard over a chest of gold. However, no trace of this has ever been found.

Gisborough Priory.
Source: Prioryman

21st

Curd tarts, known as cheesecakes, feature often in the customs of this book and were a very popular treat in the past. They differ from the cheesecakes we know today, as they more closely resemble cold tarts.

Ingredients

- 225g shortcrust pastry
- 225g curds
- 85g butter
- 55g white sugar
- 2 eggs, separated
- ½ teaspoon grated nutmeg
- one lemon peel, grated
- 55g currants

Method

- Line individual small baking tins with the shortcrust pastry
- Beat the egg whites until stiff
- Beat the butter with the sugar, then add the curds and egg yolks. Mix well
- Stir in the peel, nutmeg, and dried fruit
- Fold in the beaten egg whites
- Bake in a moderate oven for 30 minutes

22nd

There are hundreds of ways to prepare a pig, and each region probably had its own way of preserving meat for later use. The York ham originated in the nineteenth century and, though it has declined somewhat in popularity in recent years, was a beloved Yorkshire meat. Cured for anytime between three months and three years, its distinctive firm texture and salty taste made it an instant hit. Although there is one legend which states that it was created when pork was smoked on the fires of burning wood in York Minster, it was actually created by Robert Burrow Atkinson at his butcher's shop in York.

A Yorkshire pig. Source: Shutterstock

23rd

Marie Hartley and Joan Ingilby, recording ordinary life in West Yorkshire, captured a snapshot of the traditional fun and games children would have in the narrow, cobbled streets of industrial towns and cities:

> The street was our playground, and the flagged streets provided plenty of scope. Children tilluped (a hop then a stride) light-heartedly along them, or went 'hop a dock' with one foot on and one in the gutter. Chalk marks for hopscotch covered them, and children cried 'In a nick, out of the nick', as they sped along avoiding the cracks. On hot summer days globules of tar exuded between the stone setts of the roads, and when covered with fine dust and rolled into small balls they made temporary playthings.

24th

This book contains many stories about fairies, and one holds that a plucky Yorkshireman came across a group of them dancing whilst out for a walk. He decided to take one home as a present for his children. He scooped it up and put it in his pocket, but, when he got home, he found that it had disappeared!

25th

S. Baring-Gould, writing in the 1870s, described an interesting character known as Old John Mealy Face, who has since entered folklore as an archetype of Yorkshire tight-fistedness. He was born in Topcliffe on this day in 1784.

> He obtained [his nickname] by this means: John was a close-fisted old man, who stinted himself, and his wife above all, in every possible way, for he dearly loved money. He did not allow his wife enough food, and she, poor thing, was wont, when he was out for the day at market or at fair, to bake herself a loaf from which she could cut a hunch when hungry. Her husband found this out, and was very wroth. When he went to market he pressed his face down in the flour at the top of the bin, and on his return put his face back in the depressions, to make sure that the flour had not been disturbed.

On another occasion, Mealy-Face was about to be married for the third time, and said to the vicar: 'I'm an owd customer, soa, vicar, I hope ye'll do t' job cheap. Strike off two-thirds, as it's the third wife.' He died at the age of eighty-four in 1868 and was buried in Topcliffe.

26th*

The Wilson Run, or Ten Mile, is a traditional ten-mile long cross-country run held at the end of the Lent term each year at Sedburgh School. Created in 1881, it is named after Bernard Wilson, a beloved housemaster who encouraged the pupils to explore the countryside around them and build personal character through a uniquely tough physical challenge. When he died in 1913, the race was named in his honour.

27th

At Newton Kyme, near Tadcaster, is an interesting well known as Black Tom's Well. Named after Sir Thomas Fairfax, the Parliamentarian commander during the Civil War, legend has it that he hid by the well whilst pursued – presumably after the Battle of Tadcaster in 1642, when Fairfax was forced to retreat. The well is said to be haunted by his fear, and strange noises have been reported coming from it.

28th*

Palm Sunday was often known as Fig Sunday, as it was customary to eat figs. This is a reference to the stories of Jesus and the fig tree as he approached Jerusalem on Palm Sunday.

The 28th of March is also the feast of St Alkelda, of whom almost nothing is known and whose very existence is in doubt. The legend states that she was a Saxon princess who was strangled with a scarf by a Viking woman, and buried underneath the nave of St Mary and St Alkelda's church in Middleham. The only other church in the country named after her is in Giggleswick. There is a St Alkelda's Well at Middleham, and though some have suggested a connection between her name and various holy wells, this has been challenged in recent years.

29th

Kipper smoking is a traditional aspect of Whitby cuisine, and by far the most famous place is Fortune's. Established in 1872, it has used the same method to smoke kippers for over 140 years. Herring is hung over a fire and smoked for 18 hours, thus creating a unique flavour which has become a beloved snack at the seaside town.

Fortune's of Whitby. Source: Catherine Warr

30th

A famous Yorkshire folktale is that of Brother Jucundus. As the story goes, he was a fat, jovial monk who always loved good food and plenty of it. Why he became a monk was never known, but after years of simple food (and not much of it), he began to pine for his old life. He lived at St Leonard's Priory, which was right next door to St Mary's Abbey. One day he was in bed when he heard the sounds of a fair outside. He decided that he had to escape and join in the fun outside. He stole some money from the alms-box and crept out of the priory. He had immense fun at the fair – eating, drinking, and sat on a see-saw singing 'In dulci jubilo, up, up, up we go!' as he went up and down.

But his revelry was broken when he spotted two monks from the priory watching him. He careened off the see-saw, singing 'In dulci jubilo, down, down, down we go!' The monks quickly picked him up, placed him in a wheelbarrow, and took him back to the monastery. There he received a good telling-off from the Prior, for he had clearly broken the rules of the monastery. When asked to defend himself, Brother Jucundus, having consumed a good quantity of ale, simply fell back into the wheelbarrow and starting singing 'In dulci jubilo' again. This was enough – his actions had brought shame on the monastery. He was sentenced to death. The monks led him down to the cellar, with Jucundus obliviously singing 'down, down, down we go' as they went.

They put him in a cellar and gave him bread and water before starting to brick up the wall. Soon the cellar was bricked up from floor to ceiling, and Jucundus was surely to die in his little cell. When they had all gone he started throwing himself against the wall, and miraculously it gave way! He tumbled into St Mary's next door.

But little did he know that if life was bad in St Leonard's, it was much worse in St Mary's. They kept silent for 364 days of the year – they were only allowed to speak on Easter Sunday – and so nobody asked him any questions. His bed was harder, the food was smaller and tasteless, and soon he began to lose the chubbiness he'd had in St Leonard's.

A year later, the monk in charge of the cellar died and Jucundus was given his role. When the fair came round again, this time he couldn't go out, but instead crept into the cellar and helped himself to the finest communion wine. He had one glass, then another, and another, and soon lost count of how many glasses he had had. Meanwhile, the monks were impatiently waiting upstairs for their daily ration of ale. The Abbot, furious, strode into the cellar to find Brother Jucundus laying against a cask of wine and merrily swinging his glass in the air as he sang 'In dulce jubilo, up, up, up we go!'

Though it was not Easter Day, the offence was so great that it warranted a breaking of the vow of silence. It was quickly agreed that Jucundus was to be excommunicated and bricked up in the cellar to die. There was a convenient hole in one of the walls, and a great deal of loose stone, so they put him in and bricked up the wall, giving him bread and water. But Jucundus just kept singing merrily!

At the same time, a monk from his old monastery was in the cellar to collect some wine when he heard Jucundus singing. He froze. Jucundus had been dead for a year! He rushed up to the rest of the monks, who were grieving for the Prior who had recently died. They reluctantly followed him into the cellar, where they, too, heard the singing. They could not believe it! They raced for pickaxes and began to demolish the wall, and there, to the wonder and amazement of all, was Brother Jucundus! It was a miracle! With one united voice the monks proclaimed Jucundus as the new Prior, and so he lived out the rest of his days in happiness and peace.

Willy Howe Neolithic round barrow. Source: Wikimedia Commons

31st

One of the most famous fairy stories is that of the fairies at Willy Howe, in East Yorkshire. Willy Howe is a large barrow, and the story goes that in the twelfth century a man was riding late at night nearby when he heard soft and delightful music playing. Approaching it carefully, he saw a magnificent hall where a number of fairies were feasting within. He was offered a cup but, knowing the danger of eating or drinking anything offered by fairies, instead seized it and escaped from the barrow. The cup was later given to Henry I, who then sent it to his brother-in-law David, King of Scotland.

1st

Today is April Fool's Day, and an apt day to discuss 'fakelore'. One must always be careful, when researching and studying folklore, to not fall victim to spurious or invented elements which are often presented as or taken to be genuine. The most famous example of this in Yorkshire are the Cottingley Fairies. Two girls, aged 16 and 9, posed for photographs amid dancing fairies and it took Britain by storm. Even Sir Arthur Conan Doyle, the celebrated author of Sherlock Holmes, believed them to be genuine. However, in the 1980s, it was revealed that the photographs were actually faked using cardboard cut-outs.

Interestingly, such is the power of belief that, when spiritualist Edward Gardner visited the girls in 1921, he claimed to have seen dozens of fairies – even when the girls themselves said they didn't see any.

The Cottingley Fairies were made by cutting out these illustrations from *Princess Mary's Gift Book*, published in 1914, drawing on wings, and pinning them to trees. Source: Wikimedia Commons

2nd*

Good Friday was a very superstitious day, and it was believed unlucky to start any new work, write a letter, knit, lay a keel, launch a ship, begin the harvest, cut finger-nails, start a journey, get married, or give birth! In Whitby, it was believed that clothes which were hung out to dry on Good Friday would be taken down spotted with blood.

Children would often go round from house to house begging for 'pace eggs'. Deriving from the word 'paschal', meaning Easter, these eggs were hard boiled and then decorated. Sometimes a play was performed, often featuring St George triumphing over his foes, which has been revived in Calderdale. Other pace egg activities included egg-shackling, in which eggs were shaken together in a sieve and the last one to crack was the winner, and throwing them up in the air and paying a forfeit if you dropped one.

This was also a day to collect hazel sticks, which would be used to make home-made 'besoms', or brooms.

A revival of the pace-egg play at Heptonstall. Source: Averil Shepherd

3rd

One day the vicar of a parish near Yarm, as recorded by Rev. M. C. F. Morris in 1892, noticed a number of hazel sprigs and catkins stuck into various objects around the fire-place in his kitchen. When he asked the servant why she had done this, she said that it was good for the sheep at lambing time.

4th*

In Beverley Minster, Easter Sunday is announced by a choir singing hymns from the top of the north-west tower, a tradition started in 1876 by the organist and choirmaster.

Rev. M. C. F. Morris recorded that it was customary for farm lads, on Easter morning, to fill a bucket with water and place it so that the sun was reflected in it. If the sun 'glimmered' on the water, it was believed, then it would be wet on that day, and if it shone bright and clear it would be fine. It was also believed that if it was fair for the whole of Easter Day, then the following harvest would be good.

It was also common, starting from Easter Sunday noon to the following noon, to steal each other's shoes and ask a price for their return. This was often quite an intense activity, as Morris recorded that, on one occasion, 'The rector's rather dandy pupil had his coat torn right up from skirt to collar when he attempted to walk through the village on the evening'!

In Whitby, baked custard tarts were common. Perhaps originating from 'coastward', the cold, easterly winds which would sweep in from the sea were sometimes known as 'custard winds'. The Calder Valley would make dock pudding out of Passion dock, and even hold competitions to determine the best one. Also popular in summer, you can find a recipe for dock pudding on 6th June.

If your pace-egg had survived the rigours of the previous days, it was customary to roll them down a hill. If it managed to reach the bottom intact, it was seen as a sign of good luck for the rest of the year. They were also struck against each other – rather like conkers – until one was broken, known as jauping.

5th*

Every three years on Easter Monday, in the village of Barwick-in-Elmet in West Yorkshire, the maypole is taken down to be refurbished. Standing at 86ft tall, it is the second highest maypole in the UK, and a popular celebration has grown up around the whole process. As Steve Roud describes:

> The whole operation was previously carried out through a combination of brute strength and skill, with ropes and ladders, and scores of men providing the muscle, all coordinated by an elected Pole Master shouting his orders. But modern safety rules now insist that cranes and hard hats are the order of the day, which is organized by the Barwick-in-Elmet Maypole Trust. Once down, the pole is transported to a field on the shoulders of a hundred volunteers, where the renovation is carried out.

It is then decorated with flowers and garlands – including six thousand rosettes! – and repainted. On Spring Bank Holiday it is erected again amid Morris dancing, bands, and the election of a Maypole Queen. The ceremony is finished when 'a local climbs up the pole to release the ropes and, if he is brave enough, he ascends to the top and gives the weathervane a swing'. It was held on this day in 2017.

Another event is the Gawthorpe Coal Carrying race, which challenges competitors to sprint whilst carrying a sack of coal. What started in 1963 as a pub conversation between three men over who was the fittest has since grown

The Barwick-in-Elmet maypole, Source: Catherine Warr

into a hugely popular event. Men must carry 50kg of coal (women carry 20kg) over a distance of a thousand yards, and the winner is the first to drop their bag of coal at the maypole on the village green.

6th

Every farmer would need to count his sheep during lambing time, and Dales farmers often used a unique counting system known as 'Yan-Tan-Tethera'. Though the words used varied from dale to dale, they generally followed the same format. The numbers for 1 to 20 used in Swaledale, for example, were:

1 Yan	11 Yanadick
2 Tan	12 Tanadick
3 Tether	13 Tetheradick
4 Mether	14 Metheradick
5 Pip	15 Bumfit
6 Azer	16 Yanabum
7 Sezar	17 Tanabum
8 Akker	18 Tetherabum
9 Conter	19 Metherabum
10 Dick	20 Jiggit

Also used to count stiches in knitting, it fell out of use by the early nineteenth century. Though it is difficult to establish their precise origin, it is believed that they are descended from the Brythonic language, which was spoken by Celts all over the British Isles prior to the development of languages like Welsh, Cornish, etc. This is due to similarities in the words used in Yan-Tan-Tethera to other words in the Brythonic languages.

Image source: Shutterstock

7th

It was a common belief across the British Isles that fairies could swap human babies for children of their own, known as changelings. Rev. Thomas Parkinson, writing in 1889, recorded that:

> Near Grassington there is a hole in the rock, or cave, still known as 'The Fairy Hole', and for many years there resided in the town a poor deformed woman who was regarded, by many of her neighbours, as having been in her infancy a fairy changeling, and, it is to be feared, she was frequently treated accordingly.

Those born with disabilities were often seen as changelings, and this passage gives us a rather sobering insight into how disabled people were treated in the past.

Fairy Hole, Grassington cc-by-sa/2.0 - © David Rogers - geograph.org.uk/p/6109658

8th

The Ilkley White Wells were once a popular spa bath. In 1791, an advert placed in the *Leeds Intelligencer* claimed that the bath had:

> Medical qualities, famous for the cure of tumours and sores proceeding from scrophilia and other disorders – recommended for – bad eyes – the spine – or the constitution enervated.

By 1815 the baths had grown so popular that a full-time bathman was employed, and he claimed to have seen a rather fantastical sight when opening up one morning. As he turned the key in the lock, he noticed that it seemed to melt, and when he opened the door he saw:

> All over the water and dipping into it was a lot of little creatures dressed in green from head to foot, none of them more than eighteen inches high, and making a chatter and a jabber thoroughly unintelligible. They seemed to be taking a bath, only they bathed with all their clothes on. Soon however, one or two of them began to make off, bounding over the walls like squirrels. Finding they were all making ready for decamping, and wanting to have a word with them, he shouted at the top of his voice – indeed he declared afterwards he couldn't find anything else to say or do – 'Hello there!' Then away the whole tribe went, helter skelter, toppling and tumbling, head over heels, heels over head, and all the while making a noise not unlike that of a disturbed nest of young partridges. The sight was so unusual, that he declared he either couldn't or daren't attempt to rush after them … When the well had got quite clear of these strange beings he ran to the door and looked to see where they had fled, but nothing was to be seen. He ran back into the bath to see if they had left anything behind; but there was nothing; the water lay still and clear just as he had left it the previous night.

9th

Using leeches to bleed patients was common in medicine, but the job of collecting them was not a particularly glamorous one. Usually collected in the spring or summer, as leeches would not be active in the water in winter, collectors would wade through bogs and marshes with bare legs, waiting for leeches to latch on and start sucking. When enough had been gathered, the leeches would be removed and stored for later use. Bedale has an unusual leech house, which stored leeches and kept them alive prior to being sold to doctors and apothecaries. It dates from the late eighteenth or early nineteenth century and was still in use until 1900.

The leech house at Bedale. Source: Catherine Warr

10th

St Mungo's Well in Copgrove, near Harrogate, was once renowned for its healing properties. Sir John Flogers, writing in 1697, wrote that 'the people resort here to be recovered of fixed pains with or without tumour, rheumatism; quartans, strains, bruises, rickets and all weaknesses of the nerves etc.' At one time the number of people visiting the well became such a nuisance to the owners that they blocked it off! However, the water managed to break through several times and they were forced to re-open it.

11th

Pepper-cake, together with cheese and caudle (a hot, thick, milk-based drink for the sick and new mothers) was often shared out with visitors after the birth of a child. It was believed that the child would grow up without personal charms if all present did not partake of it. You can find a recipe for pepper-cake on 11th May.

12th

York Mayne Bread was a rich and spicy cross between a biscuit and a bread, traditionally presented to Royalty or any other visitors of high standing. It was last presented to Charles I, but afterwards fell into obscurity. In 2013, Dr Almute Grohmann-Sinz, working in the York archives, created a recipe based on references to the bread found in the civic records.

Ingredients

- 335g strong plain flour
- 225g sugar
- 1 teaspoon coriander
- 1 teaspoon caraway seeds

- 2 teaspoons rose water
- 3 egg yolks
- 2 egg whites
- 1 teaspoon dried yeast, or 10g fresh yeast
- ¼ pint warm water and milk, mixed

Method
- Mix together the flour, sugar and seeds
- In a basin add the rose water and 3 egg yolks
- In another basin beat the egg whites until stiff
- In yet another basin mix the yeast, warm water and milk
- Merge all the ingredients and leave to rise in a warm place for 20–30 minutes
- Roll out the dough, cut to the shapes required, and add designs to the surface
- Leave to rise again for 10 minutes and bake in a moderate oven for 10–15 minutes until golden brown.

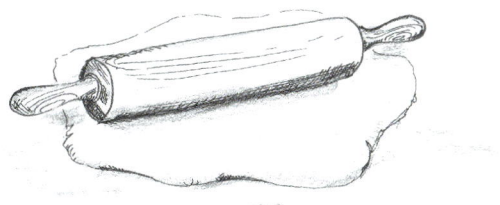

13th

Gormire lake is one of the few natural lakes in Yorkshire, and it has a number of legends associated with it. One is that a witch, when chased across the moor, took a running jump and landed in the lake. She was taken into an underwater current and emerged in a well nine miles away. There is also said to be a lost village under the water, which is likely a reference to the lost town of Semerwater (see 31st January). In another story, a goose landed in the lake and, like the witch, was sucked into the underwater currents; it then found itself in Kirkbymoorside, twelve miles away, and featherless.

14th

There is recorded, in York's official court records, a story of murder and justice from beyond the grave which happened on the 14th of April 1690. This is interesting as it shows us how seriously Yorkshire people took supernatural affairs – to the point where visions of ghosts were recorded in official court depositions.

On that day, William Barwick, from Cawood, was walking with his pregnant wife Mary through the countryside. They crossed a bridge and came to a field in which there was a pond. For some unknown reason, William suddenly grabbed his wife and threw her into the pond, holding her down until she drowned. He then took her body and hid it in the rushes before going home. Later, he returned to the site and buried her by the pond.

The next day, he visited his brother-in-law (named Thomas) at Rufforth, and told him that Mary had gone to stay with his uncle at Selby and would be there for some time. Thomas gave no thought to this. However, exactly a week later, Thomas was collecting water for his garden at a pond when he saw a woman who looked remarkably like his sister-in-law gliding towards him. He was shocked but didn't immediately think it was a ghost. She seated herself on a bank beside the pond, and there he recognised the face as that of Mary; it was 'deadly pale, the lips bloodless, the teeth showing, and the eyes fixed on something white, which he thought was a bag at the time, but afterwards supposed to be a baby'. He quickly returned to his yard and looked to see if the figure was still there – but she had vanished!

That evening he told his wife, and she urged him to visit the uncle who William said Mary was staying with. This he did the next day and, seeing that Mary was not there, went to the Lord Mayor of York to obtain an arrest warrant. William was apprehended and promptly confessed before the Mayor. He was imprisoned in York Castle, and tried and convicted in September that year. He was hanged and his body hung in chains by the pond where the murder had been committed.

15th*

Royal Maundy is a tradition which has been performed every Maundy Thursday since 1210. The monarch, or other royal, distributes alms to the needy, and it was first performed on this day by King John, who donated garments, forks, food, and other gifts to the poor of Knaresborough.

16th

A. Smith, who was born in Sheffield in the 1930s, recalled that, to cure earache, a warm onion was put into his ear and kept in place with a scarf tied round his head!

17th

The 'Celebrated Yorkshire Relish', produced in Leeds by Goodall, Backhouse & Co., was once the highest selling bottled sauce in the Victorian era. Advertised as 'the most delicious sauce in the world', many housewives tried to make their own version. Here is one recipe from 1926:

Ingredients

- ¼ pint vinegar
- 10g cayenne pods
- 10g pickling spice
- Orange juice
- Pinch of salt
- 4 teaspoons pearl barley

Method

- Mix all together, bring to boil, and simmer for 30 minutes.

Yorkshire Relish. Source: Alamy

18th

This time of year is the usual start of the English cricket season, and William Swain, who was born in Wharfedale in 1827 and later became a professional cricketer for Oxford University and Richmond, wrote the poem 'The Richmondshire Cricketers' in celebration of the time when the England team visited Richmond in 1857. It has since become a popular cricketing song.

> Ye cricketers of Richmondshire,
> Just list to what I say,
> Don on your cricket toggery,
> For England comes to-day;
> Gird well your loins as on the course
> You stand and plaudits meet –
> Prepare you for the tug of war,
> The race is on the fleet.
>
> *Chorus*
>
> Then bowl away my jolly boys,
> With bias, break or spin,
> And show these noble champions
> That Richmondshire can win.
>
> Success to all you racing blades,
> What horses ere were fleeter?
> There's Abdale with Vedette and Skrim,
> And Watson with good Sneta
> He showed them how the race to win –
> John Scott with Mare so famous –
> For Imperieuse came in the first,
> And beat the Ignoramus.
>
> Then to the field once more return,
> Let cricket be the fashion,
> And talk about the England match,
> And have no more digression.
> Let one and all, at duty's call,

Contrive to buy a ticket,
And come to see the Richmond gents,
Against England play at cricket.

The bowler then for England,
Martingell, Willisher, and Jackson
Davies, King, Anderson, Hayward,
Clark, and Downs for action:
With Mr Hirst, whose name's the first,
There Dr. Parr so clever,
He swallowed a box of his uncle's pills,
And is going to score for ever.

In stepping out to hit a ball,
Suppose it be short 'un,
You'll find your reign cut very short
By Stephenson or Morton,
Whose sole talent you'll quickly see,
If you happen just to snitch it,
They'll catch, or stump, and say 'how's that?'
And thus you'll lose your wicket.

So may we see a glorious match,
With the twenty-two in favour,
The England men may win the game,
But Richmonshire I'd rather,
Success to all who field and bowl,
And those who guard the wicket,
And all those who want good health
Must come and play at cricket.

Image source:
Shutterstock

19th

Haverah Park lies about three miles west of Harrogate, and its creation story is as follows: there once was a cripple named Haverah who lived in Knaresborough. One day, he came across John of Gaunt, who owned a large amount of land in the area, and begged him for some land to farm. John of Gaunt replied:

> I, John o' Gaunt,
>
> Do give and do grant
>
> To thee, Haverah,
>
> As much of my ground
>
> As thou canst hop round
>
> On a long summer day.

Haverah gladly accepted, and set about hopping around the land as fast as he could. The space of land which he covered has since been known as Haverah Park.

Remains of John O'Gaunt's castle at Haverah Park.
Source: Wikimedia Commons

20th

One popular story is that of the drummer boy of Richmond. For many years it was rumoured that there were subterranean passages from Richmond Castle to the town, and this is a key element in the story of Potter Thompson (see 14th October). One day, a group of soldiers believed that there was a tunnel from the castle to Easby Abbey, and so rather than risking exploring the tunnel themselves, they found a boy who was small enough and asked him to do it. He was a drummer boy, and he was told to simply take his drum and walk along the passage, drumming as he went. He set off, and soon the sound of drumming faded away. Then it stopped. Nobody knows exactly what happened, but the little drummer boy was never seen again. Some say that at night, when all is quiet, you can still hear his ghostly drumming.

21st*

The Fellsman Hike, a gruelling, sixty-mile long route from Ingleton to Threshfold, is held every year around this time. The oldest challenge hike in the North of England, it was started in 1962 by Don Thompson and includes some of the most challenging terrain in the area. Hikers compete for the prized Fellsman Axe as they traverse two of Yorkshire's Three Peaks – Ingleborough and Whernside.

22nd

The Devil's Punchbowl, or Hole of Horcum, is a huge hole in the highest part of the North York Moors. There are two stories associated with its origin; one is that it was scooped up by the devil, and the other is that it was made by Wade the Giant (see 3rd May), who dug up handfuls of earth to make the nearby Blakey Topping and Wade's Causeway.

23rd

Guilds dedicated to St George were popular in the country at one time, including York. (This is not to be confused with the Guild of St George created by John Ruskin.) The primary purpose of these guilds was, as Steve Roud describes:

> To provide and maintain effigies of the saint in local churches; some were even wealthy enough to build chapels dedicated to him. The effigies were carried in procession around the parish every April – as near to St George's Day as possible – and these events became one of the most spectacular and extravagant affairs in the local church calendar. Even more popular for the crowd than the saint himself was the figure of the dragon. This could be a small one made of wood and mounted on a pole (with snapping jaws worked by a string), or a more elaborate basket-work affair that men could carry from inside or wheel along. George also appeared in civic pageants, celebrating the election of a new mayor, for example, and 'riding St George' was an annual excuse for the local great and good to ride in state around the town.

This custom declined during the Reformation when statues and effigies of St George were destroyed. However, they are carried on in spirit with the introduction in recent years of St George's Day parades.

St George and the Dragon.
Source: Wikimedia Commons

24th

The Challenge Cup Final has become a staple in the Rugby League calendar, a time when fans of all clubs descend on Wembley Stadium to celebrate one of the highlights of the Rugby League season. It was first held on this day in 1897 at Headingly Stadium in Leeds, with Yorkshire club Batley defeating St Helen's 10-3 in front of a crowd of 13,492. The final has been held at Wembley since 1929, and that year also saw the introduction of another Challenge Cup Final tradition – the singing of 'Abide With Me' before the match.

This day is also St Mark's Eve, and in Yorkshire it was associated with death. It was believed that those who kept watch over the church porch from midnight until one o'clock would see the spirits of all those who were to die during the rest of the year. Those who fell asleep whilst keeping watch, it was believed, would themselves die.

25th

One day, as the story goes, the devil sought to build a bridge at Kirkby Lonsdale. He was carrying large stones in his apron over Giggleswick when the strings of his apron suddenly snapped and the rocks were sent cascading onto the ground. They are still there today, and called the Apronful of Stones.

26th

It was believed to not disturb fairies if you saw them dancing. One story from Craven tells of a man who came across a fairy dance, but deliberately avoided them. When he returned to the spot the next morning, he found that the ground was covered with mushrooms. This, his wife informed him, was a reward for not interrupting the fairy dance.

27th*

The Three Peaks Race – known as 'The Marathon With Mountains' – has been held on the last weekend in April since 1954. Traversing the Yorkshire Three Peaks of Pen-y-Ghent, Ingleborough and Whernside, it originated with three schoolteachers from Giggleswick who claimed to have completed a walking circuit in ten hours in 1887. At twenty-three miles long, it grew in popularity as a long-distance endurance race and is now a high-profile fell race which receives considerable media attention.

Ingleborough
Source: Wikimedia Commons

28th

Caedmon, who lived at Whitby Abbey during the abbacy of St Hilda (see 17th November), is the earliest English poet we know of by name and one of the most important religious poets of his time. Living in the seventh century, the story of his life has entered into the folklore of Whitby. As the legend goes, Caedmon originally cared for the animals at the Abbey and knew no songs. One night, while everyone else was feasting and singing, Caedmon left early to be with his animals as he couldn't join in with the singing. That night, in a dream, someone appeared to him and asked him to sing 'the beginning of created things'. He refused at first, but then produced a beautiful poem praising God. The next morning, having remembered everything, he was taken to see St Hilda, who was struck by the beauty of his poetry. Believing it to be a gift from God, he was asked to take monastic vows and lived out the rest of his life writing beautiful poetry as a monk.

Facing page: a cross, featuring Caedmon and St. Hilda, in the graveyard of St. Mary's Church, Whitby. Source: Catherine Warr

29th

Marie Hanson Moore, author of *A Yorkshire Cookbook*, remembers one mouth-watering local tradition:

> I lived in the West Riding of Yorkshire, in the heavy woollen district [...] One of these traditions in my town was the Thursday Baking Day. I can still remember the warm, spicy smells that greeted me upon my return from school, as I opened the door of the house and went inside our tiny living-room [...] Each Thursday, on the big table, would be spread large, golden, crisp-topped loaves of bread, enough for a week's eating, for no Yorkshire housewife would dream of buying her bread, unless in a dire emergency. There would be one large fruit-cake, redolent of cinnamon and mixed spice; trays of small buns, spotted with currants (there for my brother and his rugby-playing friends); shortcrust almond tarts, crisp and golden, with a delicious splodge of jam hidden beneath the almond mixture; saucer-sized Yorkshire curd tarts, spicy and faintly cheesy; and the large square slab of parkin, brown and sticky on top, adding its ginger scent to the rest. All this – except the parkin which was put away for a week to improve – was to be eaten the week following baking day, and sure enough, by the time it came round again, the cake tins would be empty.

30th

One Yorkshire folktale is that of a cobbler who lived at Thorpe named Ralph. He would make and repair shoes for the monks at Fountains Abbey, and his journey to the abbey would force him to ford the River Dibb as there was no bridge there. One day, when he'd sat down for a moment, he sang a song:

> As he was riding along the highway
>
> Old Nick came unto him, and thus did he say,
>
> Sing link-a-down, heigh-down, ho-down-derry.

Imagine his shock and surprise to find that, when he turned round, the devil was behind him! Ralph was terrified at first, but they soon began to chat amicably. He even shared some of his lunch with him.

'I dunno,' said the cobbler, 'If tha be t' devil or not, but if tha be, build us a brigg [bridge] ower t'beck.'

The devil rose and bowed. He vanished. All of a sudden, there appeared a bridge over the River Dibb.

Dibbles Bridge. Source: Wikimedia Commons

1st

Many villages in Yorkshire still hold traditional May Day celebrations, although many of these are no longer performed on May Day itself but rather at a more convenient weekend. These often include the traditional activities – such as maypole dancing, music, and Morris dancing – which have been practised for hundreds of years.

One of the more interesting maypole-related occurrences are the village 'maypole wars'. Neighbourly rivalries are to be expected, but sometimes these can spill out into grievous acts of maypole theft. The villages of Burnsall and Barwick-in-Elmet, for example, have both had their maypoles stolen by rival villages – though they were soon returned or replaced. Often, these can become quite emotionally charged events, with this being the reaction of Barwick-in-Elmet to receiving back their stolen maypole in 1966:

> Flags were flying from windows and many inhabitants came out to welcome it back. The pubs emptied as crowds started to fill the street. Dogs barked, young boys ran about waving their arms and a little old lady cried. The pole was well guarded for the remaining two days and raised in a very successful ceremony on Whit Tuesday as planned.

The elaborate process of replacing the Barwick-in-Elmet maypole can be found on 5th April.

2nd*

This day is known as Spaw Sunday. Held on the first Sunday in May, it is unique to Yorkshire and Lancashire. It focuses on local holy wells, where it is believed that the waters only hold healing properties on that particular day. The waters are blessed by clergy before the crowd take turns to smell or taste the water, which is usually highly sulphurous. It was also traditional to mix the water with liqourice in order to sweeten the taste. In Calderdale, dock pudding is served at events, and despite the tradition nearly dying out in the twentieth century, it has been successfully revived.

Since 1880, a cricket match has been sporadically played at Ilkley between the White Hats and the Black Hats. Originally a competition between shopkeepers and tradesmen, it died out in 1994 before being revived in recent years. The rules are pretty much 'anything goes', as players have previously arrived on donkeys, had an unlimited number of players on each team, and even used broomsticks for bats! Teams compete for the original 1880 silverware, and it is currently played on May Bank Holiday Monday as part of the Ilkley Carnival. It was held on this day in 2017.

3rd

Wade is a legendary giant who appears across the folklore of various cultures and has a number of associations with Yorkshire. One story is that he and his wife Bell built Mulgrave Castle and Pickering Castle and would throw a hammer to each other over the hills. In another, he built a road for Bell to take her cow to market or pasture, and this is known as Wade's Causeway. One day, his son was growing impatient for his milk and hurled a huge stone to where Bell was milking her cow on the moors. When it hit her, it broke off and could still be seen on the moors for many years.

Wade's Causeway. Source: Wikimedia Commons

4th*

The first Saturday in the month is the occasion for the Gawthorpe May Day celebrations. As Steve Roud describes:

> A procession involving themed floats, bands, children in fancy dress, and the local May Queen takes place, and there is also plaited maypole dancing, of which Gawthorpe is particularly proud, performed by schoolgirls from the village. The event has been organised by the Maypole Committee since 1874, but this was merely a formalisation of an older tradition of maypoles in the village. In 1850 [...] inter-village rivalry got out of hand when men from nearby Chickenley undertook a raid and sawed part-way through the pole; in the ensuing fight, one man died and many were injured. The wind finished off that particular pole not long after, but there have been others since.

5th*

Today is the feast of St Ecca of Crayke, an Anglo-Saxon priest and hermit who lived in the village of Crayke in North Yorkshire. Most of what we know about him is from a poem written by St Alcuin of York (*c*.735–804):

> Then flourished Echa, venerable man,
> A holy anchorite in wilderness;
> A secret life he sought, and in chaste zeal
> Fled from all earthly honours, that,
> With God His King, he might find honours at heaven's court;
> Devoutly led on Earth an angel's life,
> And seem'd as if with prophetic pow'r inspired.

St. Cuthbert's, Crayke. The body of St. Cuthbert is said to have been taken here for a time to escape from Danish invaders. Source: Catherine Warr

6th

'Efter lambing time, yer started on at peeat,' recalled one dales farmer born in 1885. 'It was a job to be done just like haymaking. Ivvery hamlet 'ed its own peeat pot i'them days.'

Peat, or turf, was for centuries the chief fuel used in the dales. Each house in a village would have its own plot of peat on the moor or common where they were free to extract the fuel. Collected in late spring and early summer, it was a free (and plentiful) alternative to coal.

7th

Today is the feast day of St John of Beverley, a highly important religious figure in the seventh and eighth centuries who founded the town of Beverley and was at one time a member of the Whitby religious community with St Hilda (see 17th November). John was canonised in 1037, and belief in the miracles associated with him was one of the reasons why Beverley prospered. On the day of the Battle of Agincourt it was said that blood and oil ran from his tomb, showing that John had miraculously intervened to secure Henry V victory in battle.

On the Sunday nearest to the 7th of May – the feast of St John of Beverley – civic dignitaries process in full regalia to Beverley Minster. Children from Harpham, the birthplace of St John, place primroses from the village around his tomb.

8th

I. Hinton, writing for *The Dalesman* in 1971, recalled his teenage years in Rotherham as a miner during the General Strike of 1926. Between the 4th and 12th May, over a million and a half workers downed tools in protest against falling wages and poor working conditions. He describes playing a variation of the popular game Knurr-and-Spell (see February 6).

> We played [...] Nippsy. Nippsy is a similar game except the striker is a pick-handle, and the nippsy a small piece of wood specially designed to rise from the floor when hit at one end, and again to be knocked as far as possible.

9th*

On the Thursday nearest to the feast of John of Beverley (7th May), the choir and congregation of Beverley Minster attend church at Harpham and process to the holy well of St John there, which is decorated with flowers. After praying and singing hymns, they return to the church for choral evensong.

St John's Well, Harpham.
Image copyright: R. B. Parish

10th

Quoits is a traditional game which is still played in some parts of Yorkshire. The aim is to throw a 'quoit' – a ring of metal, like a hollowed-out discus – onto a stake which sticks out from the ground. The stake (called a pin in Yorkshire) is set in the middle of a square bed of clay, and players score points through a variety of methods involving the quoit and the pin. This deceptively simple game has something of a minor cult following, and even has its own governing body – The National Quoits Association.

Quoits. Source: Wikimedia Commons

11th

Contrary to its title, pepper-cake does not actually contain any pepper. Also eaten at Christmas time, it was traditionally given to new mothers along with caudle and shared out with those present (see 11th April).

Ingredients

- 700g plain flour
- 225g butter
- 225g dark brown sugar
- 28g ground cloves
- 1 teaspoon bicarbonate of soda
- 700g black treacle
- 4 large eggs
- A little milk

Method

- Rub the butter into the flour and stir in the ground cloves and the sugar
- Beat the eggs well and add to the mixture with the treacle
- Dissolve the bicarbonate of soda in half a teacup of milk and add to the mix
- Stir well, adding a more milk if necessary.
- Put the mix into a greased and lined cake tin
- Bake in a moderate oven for around 90 minutes. Test with a skewer to see if it comes out clean. If it does, it's ready.

12th*

On the morning of Ascension Eve in Whitby, a hedge of sticks and branches is built near the water's edge. Called a Penny Hedge, it was first built in 1159 and is said to have originated from the time when a hermit gave refuge to a hunted boar, only to be killed by three hunters when they followed it. Before he died, the hermit forgave them – but only on the condition that the hunters perform penance by building a hedge on the sands each year. From the original 'Penance hedge' we then, over time, got the name 'Penny hedge'.

On the second Sunday in May each year since 1927, hundreds of cyclists have gathered at the village of Coxwold, near Thirsk, for a special service at St Michael's Church. Known as 'Coxwold Sunday', it is a service of remembrance for cyclists who have lost their lives and a celebration of the Cyclists' Touring Club and the sport in general.

Constructing the Penny Hedge at Whitby. Source: Wikimedia Commons

13th

A common way to cure croup in infants was to rub goose fat on the chest or back, then cover with brown paper or cloth. Similarly, pneumonia could be cured with a bread poultice applied to the chest.

14th

Marie Hartley and Ella Pontefract, in their journey through the dales during the 1940s, recorded a delightful local custom in the village of Keld, in Swaledale:

> Twice a year the people make some effort to pay for the upkeep of the village hall. In the spring they have what they call a 'May Stir', and at the beginning of November an 'Autumn Stir', generally a concert with a supper and dance to follow. The local women do the catering. For a week beforehand the delicious smells waft out of cottage doors, and you find the women, busy and rather heated, rolling and beating, and opening oven doors. They count in stones, not dozens. One will promise to make up a stone of flour into tarts, another into cakes, another into bread. There is something delightfully natural about it all, a communal idea which spreads the interest. Those who have promised to bake call in one or two other women to help, so that for many the excitement of the event begins a week before.

15th

It was believed unlucky for a hen to crow, and sometimes the unlucky bird was killed afterwards as it was thought it would bring nothing but misfortune to the household. Hence the old saying: 'A crowing hen and a whistling maid both bring bad luck.'

16th

The custom of 'chalking' each other was apparently common in the Bridlington area, as seen in this 1890 report:

> At Bridlington, on the Sunday night preceding the fair, which is held on the Monday before Whit Sunday, the boys used to assemble on the Church Green, where the fair was held, each armed with a lump of chalk, and each intent on chalking the backs of as many of the other boys as possible. This often led to quarrels, as the boys then had on their Sunday clothes.

17th

One very famous Yorkshire folktale is that of the Dragon of Loschy Wood. As the story goes, there once lived a great dragon in Loschy Wood, near Nunnington. He terrorised the villages and slew many knights who tried to kill it. One day a knight named Peter Loschy, with his trusty dog, came to the village. He went to the blacksmith and ordered a set of armour which had spikes and sharp blades all over the outside. He approached the dragon, and when it tried to wrap its long body around him and squash him like a boa constrictor, it cut itself on his armour. However, no matter how many times Peter stabbed it, the dragon only needed to roll on the ground and it would be healed. It was then that he whistled for his dog, so that whenever he chopped off a limb, the dog would pick it up and carry it away. In this way the dragon could not heal itself, and soon the entire dragon had been chopped up into little bits and slain. The dog leapt up and licked the knight's face, but, unbeknownst to him, the blood of the dragon was poisonous, and Peter soon died. His dog died of a broken heart soon afterwards, and in the church at Nunnington there is a tomb of a knight in armour, with a dog at his feet.

18th*

The Antient Silver Arrow Contest is reputed to be the oldest and longest running sporting event in the world. First held in 1673 in Scorton, North Yorkshire, anyone over the age of 21 is allowed to take part shooting traditional bows, and the winner is the first to hit the centre of the target. The winner then takes on the responsibility of organising next year's contest.

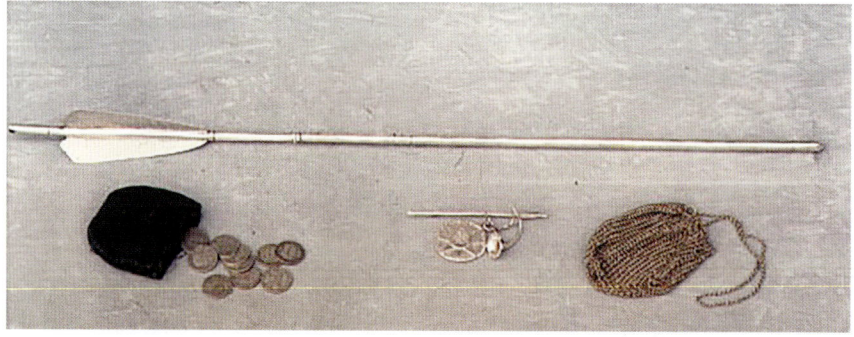

The Antient Scorton Silver Arrow, held at the Royal Armories in Leeds. A replica is given as a prize each year. With kind permission from the Society of Archers © Society of Archers

The Saturday before the Spring Bank Holiday weekend in May is also the occasion for the Otley Show – the oldest one-day agricultural show in the country. The first event in the country show calendar, it attracts thousands of visitors each year and showcases livestock, machinery, and a variety of country crafts. The oldest recorded show was held in 1796, but it is believed that some were held before this date.

19th

Although the keeping of bees in ordinary households has largely died out, it is still possible to find 'bee boles', which are holes in garden or dry-stone walls where simple beehives were housed. Bees normally swarm around this time in the summer, and they were valued immensely because honey was used as the main sweetener before sugar became widely available to the general public. The bees themselves were often highly valued, too, and sometimes even considered a part of the family; when a member of a family in Gamsworth in Wharfedale died, the bees were put into mourning. It was thought that if they were not told, they would never do any more good.

Bee Boles. Source: Shutterstock

20th

Rev. M. C. F. Morris, writing in 1892, recorded some wedding traditions common at one time in Yorkshire:

> The customs connected with marriage festivities have changed a good deal of late years. The old custom, for instance, of running races for ribbons is not so prevalent as it was when I was a boy, and as I remember it in the East Riding, when the races used to be run by the young men down the 'town street', generally immediately after the marriage service at the church was concluded. Sometimes it used to be arranged that the races should finish at the house of the bride's father. The prize was nearly always a ribbon or ribbons, very commonly a white one as representing the bride, and coloured ones similarly the bridesmaids. Now-a-days, where the traditional custom is still kept up, scarves or handkerchiefs are frequently substituted for ribbons. It was a proud moment for the victor on these occasions, and many a man will recount with delight and elation the number of ribbons he has won in such contests.

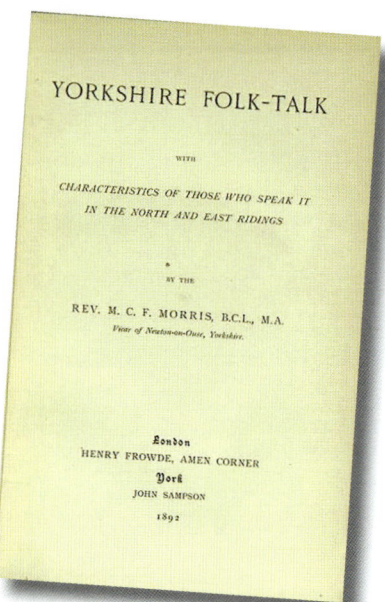

21st

Although well dressing – a custom in which wells and springs are decorated with designs made from flowers – is concentrated mostly in Derbyshire, it has been known to be practised in Yorkshire. Booming during the eighteenth and nineteenth centuries, it fell out of use before being revived in the 1950s. In 2008 it was performed at Penistone, near Barnsley.

An example of well-dressing. Source: Catherine Warr

22nd

Harrogate Tart is a very old Yorkshire dish which was once extremely popular. This recipe dates from 1900.

Ingredients

- Shortcrust pastry, enough to fill a flan case
- *For the filling*
- 3 egg yolks
- 1 tablespoon cold milk
- 1 pint hot milk
- 28g butter
- 1 whole egg, beaten
- 85g plain flour
- 85g caster sugar
- 113g ground almonds

Method

- Roll out the pastry to fit the flan case, prick the bottom lightly, and bake at 200°C/400°F/gas mark 6 for around 25 minutes or until golden
- Mix the flour to a smooth paste with the cold milk, then stir in the egg yolks
- Mix in the whole beaten egg and sugar, stirring continually
- Melt the butter in the hot milk and then stir gradually into the egg mixture
- Put the mixture into a thick-sided saucepan and cook very slowly, stirring all the time, until it thickens and resembles smooth cream – do not let it boil!
- Remove from the heat and beat in the ground almonds
- Pour into the pre-baked pastry case and let it set. Dust with icing sugar and serve cold.

23rd*

Whitmonday, the Monday after Pentecost, was officially recognised as a bank holiday in 1871. This meant that, with an extra day off work, many fairs and festivals sprang up across the country to give the public a fun day out. One of these was the Bowling Fair in Bradford. A highly popular event each year, in 1897 William Scruton complained that the fair had 'altered for the worse with the coming of pea saloons, shooting galleries and fat women'!

24th

Mary Bostock, of Castle Bolton, recalled that a traditional cure for a rheumatic knee was to tie a bandage soaked in vinegar around it.

25th

Another unusual set of Yorkshire wedding customs was recorded by Rev. M. C. F. Morris:

> In some places the old custom for the bride and bridegroom on their return from the church to be presented at the door of the bride's house with a cake on a plate is still observed. The bride takes the cake and eats a portion of it, while the bridegroom lays hold of the plate and throws it behind him. The future happiness of the young couple is supposed to depend on the breaking of the plate. Sometimes the cake is cut into small pieces and thrown by the bride over her head and the plate broken. Another 'use' is for someone to meet the newly married couple at the churchyard gate carrying a live chicken. He follows the bridal procession to the bride's house, making the chicken squeak, and will not go away 'till the chicken is satisfied'.

26th

This song – 'The Yorkshire Bite' – was highly popular in Yorkshire during the early nineteenth century, the earliest printed version dating from 1782. 'Bite' was a word which meant 'trick', as the clever Yorkshire lad manages to outwit the highwayman.

If you please, do draw near, it's the truth I declare,
It was of an old farmer in Herefordshire;
He'd a fair Yorkshire boy who acted as man
To manage his business, his name they called John.

Chorus

To me fol-the-dol-lero-li-day.

One morning quite early he called up his man,
And when he came to him, as we understand,
He said, 'Take this cow to Hereford Fair;
She is in good order, I can well her spare.'

Away went the boy with his whip in his hand
And soon reached the fair as you'll all understand.
Well, in a short time he met with three men
And sold one his cow for six pounds ten.

They went to an alehouse in order to drink;
It was there that the farmer paid the boy down his chink.
The boy to the landlady then he did say,
'Oh, what shall I do with this money, I pray?'

'I will sew it within thy coat-lining,' said she,
'For fear on the road there a robber should be.'
Close by sat a highwayman drinking his wine;
Thought he to himself, 'That money is mine.'

The boy took his leave and he homeward did go,
And the highwayman soon followed after also.
He soon overtook him upon the highway,
And, 'Well overtaken, young man,' he did say.

'Will you get up behind me?' the highwayman said.
'How far are you going?' replied the lad.
'Well, it's three or four miles for what I do know.'
So he jumped up behind and away they did go.

They rode till they came to a very dark lane;
The highwayman says, 'Now I'll tell you quite plain,
Deliver up your money without noise or strife,
Or else I shall certainly take your sweet life.'

The boy soon found out there could be no dispute,
So he quickly alighted without fear or doubt;
He tore his coat linings, the money took out,
And among the long grasses he strewed it about.

The highwayman then he jumped down off his horse,
But little he thought that it was for his loss.
And before he could find any money, they say,
The boy jumped on horseback and rode fast away.

The highwayman shouted and begged him to stay;
The boy wouldn't hear him, but kept on his way,
And to his old master the boy he did bring
Horse, saddle and bridle, a very fine thing.

The master he laughed while his sides he did hold
And said, 'For a boy thou hast been very bold.
Now as for the villain, thou hast served him right
And hast put upon him a real Yorkshire bite.'

They searched in the saddle bags and quickly they told
Two-hundred pounds in silver and gold
And two brace of pistols; the boy he did vow,
'I think, good master, I've well sold the cow!'

27th*

The Richmond Meet, held every year on Spring Bank Holiday, has been entertaining the town of Richmond and raising money for good causes since 1892. Complete with a fair and a carnival procession filled with colourful floats and costumes, the Meet is a key feature of the Richmond social calendar and an enjoyable day for all.

28th

Marie Hanson Moore, in her Yorkshire cookbook, recalled one memorable childhood home remedy:

> This [snakeweed] was also a very good remedy for those spring pimples and spots. My own family cure for them was a nauseatingly throat-gagging mixture of what was called brimstone and treacle, which consisted of large spoonfuls of flowers in sulphur mixed with black treacle; the memory of it remains.

29th

Today is Oak Apple Day, which celebrates the time when Charles II escaped from the Parliamentarians by hiding in an oak tree after the Battle of Worcester in 1651. It was traditional to go around wearing sprigs of oak leaf and to beat anyone not wearing one with a bunch of nettles.

30th*

On Trinity Sunday, at the 'pea-scaldings' or 'peascod' feasts around Whitby, peas were boiled or steamed in their pods before being served at a large table. Everyone then took a pod and, dipping it into a cup of melted butter, attempted to extract the peas between their teeth.

31st

The Bellerby feast was once a popular village event, described in this 1989 account:

> The principal participants dress as clowns and, accompanied by an accordion player, drummer, and helpers, they go from door to door round the village collecting money, cakes, sweets, raffle prizes, and so on. They also stop pedestrians, passing cars, coaches, and whoever else they can find to exact contribution. The edibles are distributed to children and other villagers who gather for the purpose around midday, and the money goes to organizing a fête on the day and, later in the year, a children's disco and Christmas party. The custom has changed over the years, and was several times in danger of extinction, but local effort revived interest each time. Its date has moved from the Wednesday after Whitsun to Whit Monday (in 1933) and later to the Spring Bank Holiday. The heavy drinking previously associated with the custom has been toned down, and the event made more family oriented.

This custom sadly seems to have declined sharply in recent years.

June

1st*

One unusual local sport is that of Maltby Beckball. Four teams, with three balls, aim to score goals through four goalposts on a field which has a beck winding through the middle! It is thought to have started in the 1920s and was revived during the 1980s as part of the Maltby Festival in June. Maltby is a mining town near Rotherham, and the colliers originally played in their pit clothes and boots – although, when it was revived, more appropriate attire was chosen. The very few rules are simple: four teams (of about a dozen players each) try to defend their own goal and put a ball into another. How they do this is up to them, as a ball can be kicked, run with, punched, or thrown. Three balls are used all at the same time – one rugby and two footballs – and so the game somewhat resembles Quidditch, with multiple balls flying about (albeit with more scrambling in the mud). Those who volunteer as goalkeepers tend to save one shot, only to be bowled over a second later by another ball which passes through. Makeshift scrums often take place, usually formed by two or more teams flattening each other as they run in opposite directions after different balls. Players splash and flounder their way across the beck, which is treated as just another part of the pitch, and so the game soon descends into a mass of wet, muddy men floundering in the freshly-made bog. Every fifteen minutes the game pauses and the teams swap goals. In 1992, the final score was recorded as 21 goals to Don Jon, 15 to White Swan, 11 to Don Jon II, and 10 to Others. There was also a broken collarbone. The event had attracted a large number of spectators, who often found themselves ducking out of the way of flying balls.

2nd

Marie Hartley and Ella Pontefract, in their tour of the Yorkshire Dales in the 1940s, captured a summer village scene which is quintessentially Yorkshire:

> Keld Sports, perhaps a bigger 'stir', are another occasion for much baking. They are held in June at Rowley Bottom, a field below West Stonesdale, about half a mile above Keld. There is a true local spirit about them. The field slopes down on either side to the beck, and the people sit on one bank to watch the sheep-dog trials on the other. […] The village band plays at intervals, between which the bandsmen enter for quoits and races. The band-master has difficulty in getting them together again for the next burst of music, a round of quoits being too important to be interrupted.

3rd*

Mystery Plays, once a huge spectacle in York before being abolished in 1569, were revived for the Festival of Britain in 1951 and have proved immensely popular ever since. One of only four surviving mystery play cycles, it was traditionally held every year on the feast of Corpus Christi, however nowadays it is only held every four years and at various times of the year. These mystery plays are unusual in that, since their beginning, they have been put on *by* the people of York *for* the people of York; traditionally, each guild in the city would be responsible for performing a specific story, usually related to that guild's particular craft. For example, shipwrights would perform a play about Noah's Ark, and bakers would perform about the Last Supper. There are 48 mystery plays in the cycle, and they have sometimes featured famous actors; both Mary Ure and Dame Judi Dench played Mary whilst at school in York.

Processions would also take place in the city on the Feast of Corpus Christi, as seen in this nineteenth century description of the occasion:

A fifteenth-century Mystery Play. Source: Wikimedia Commons

On the day before and the morning of the day itself, thousands of spectators streamed into the city. On Corpus Christi morn, artisans and tradesmen rose early, spending an hour or two completing the arrangements of their large stages. At 9.a.m. the procession started, beginning to play first at the gates of the priory of the Holy Trinity then it proceeded so that every street had a pageant, 'all at one time playing together'.

4th

The Lyke Wake Dirge is a well-known traditional Yorkshire song, and although the earliest printed version dates from the seventeenth century, it likely originated much earlier. This account, from the sixteenth century, describes the practice of singing the dirge over the body of someone who had recently died:

> When any dieth, certaine women sing a song to the dead bodie, reciting the jorney that the partye deceased must goe; and they are of beliefe (such is their fondnesse) that once in their lives, it is good to give a pair of new shoes to a poor man, for as much, as after this life, they are to pass barefoote through a great launde, full of thornes and furzen, except by the meryte of the almes aforesaid they have redeemedthe forfeyte; for, at the edge of the launde, an oulde man shall meet them with the same shoes that were given by the partie when he was lyving; and, after he hath shodde them, dismisseth them to go through thick and thin without scratch or scalle.

The dirge is below, as printed in 1900:

> This ae nighte, this ae nighte,
> (Refrain): —Every nighte and alle,
> Fire and fleet and candle-lighte,
> (Refrain): And Christe receive thy saule.
>
> When thou from hence away art past,
> To Whinny-muir thou com'st at last;
> If ever thou gavest hosen and shoon,
> Sit thee down and put them on;
>
> If hosen and shoon thou ne'er gav'st nane
> The whinnes sall prick thee to the bare bane;
> From Whinny-muir when thou may'st pass,
> To Brig o' Dread thou com'st at last;

From Brig o' Dread when thou may'st pass,
To Purgatory fire thou com'st at last;
If ever thou gavest meat or drink,
The fire sall never make thee shrink;

If meat or drink thou ne'er gav'st nane,
The fire will burn thee to the bare bane;
This ae nighte, this ae nighte,
—Every nighte and alle,
Fire and fleet and candle-lighte,
And Christe receive thy saule.

5th

Rev. M. C. F. Morris, in 1892, recorded one way of finding out the identity of a thief in Yorkshire:

> One of the longest lived of these terrors to evil-doers was the custom of resorting to the Bible and key for the detection of a thief. The method was a favourite one in many parts of the country, Yorkshire not excepted. The modus operandi was this: a key was placed in a Bible, and after having been bound round tightly with string, the Bible, with the key inside, would be hung from a nail in the wall or some convenient place. The name of the suspected thief would then be repeated three times, and if the key turned in the Book, the person who had been named was declared the thief.

6th

Dock Pudding is a traditional Yorkshire recipe which is native to the Calder Valley. So beloved is the dish that a World Dock Pudding competition is held every year.

Ingredients

- Fresh young dock leaves, with stalks and large veins removed – make sure to collect the correct variety. You will need the *Persicaria Bistorta*, **not** the dock leaves used to ease nettle stings
- 2 finely chopped onions or spring onions
- 1 handful of oatmeal
- 1 small knob of butter

Method

- Wash the dock and nettle leaves well and strain
- Boil the docks, nettles and chopped onions in a little salted water until just tender
- Add 2–3 tablespoons of oatmeal and simmer the mix for 20 minutes
- Strain off excess liquid and stir in a knob of butter.
- Season with pepper and salt and fry the pudding, preferably in bacon fat.

7th

At Mount Grace Priory is St John's Well, which for many years supplied the Carthusian priory with water. It was known as a pin well, as young ladies would bend pins through ivy leaves and throw them into the water whilst making a wish. This wish must be kept secret, for if it was told to anyone it would not come true.

8th*

St William of York, whose feast day is today, was born in the city sometime in the late eleventh century. He was elected Archbishop and was involved in a number of ecclesiastical and political arguments. He rubbed shoulders with many influential figures of his day and died in 1154, allegedly after drinking from a poisoned chalice whilst holding Mass. He was buried in York Minster and within a few months of his death miracles were reported – during a fire, his body remained unsinged and a sweet smell came from his tomb. He was canonised in 1227, and his remains are still in the crypt at York Minster.

The second Saturday in June witnesses the Great Knaresborough Bed Race – a 'mighty pageant of decorated beds, passengers and runners, combined with a gruelling athletic contest around a course of 2.4 miles.' Held every year since 1966, it is a highly entertaining event which takes up to 90 teams (often in ingenious and elaborately designed beds and costumes) through the countryside and streets of Knaresborough, including through the River Nidd itself. It raises funds for charitable and community causes and is an excellent family day out.

A creative entry in the Knaresborough Bed Race. Source: Knaresborough Lions Club

9th*

The biennial walk of the Coverdale Foresters' Friendly Society takes place on the second Wednesday in June. The Coverdale Foresters are one of only a few surviving 'friendly societies', which at one time numbered hundreds in Yorkshire. In a friendly society, members would pay a subscription to cover the costs of medical care, funerals, and other necessary expenses for fellow members. In the days before government welfare, these were vital in providing aid for members of the community. Founded in 1816, the Coverdale Foresters still wear the traditional green coats, sashes, and peaked hats on their walk.

10th

Dry stone walls are one of the most iconic features of the Yorkshire landscape, and it is believed that there are over 5,000 miles of them in Yorkshire. Farmers would traditionally repair their own walls, and it was considered one of the jobs for the month of June. This is likely because the farmers had little other work to do at this time, and so could dedicate their days to the slow and intensive process of repairing and building dry stone walls. It was also the time when, if ever, they took a holiday.

Dry stone walling in the Yorkshire Dales. Source: Wikimedia Commons

11th*

Today is the feast of St Barnabas, and 'Barnaby Day' was an annual fair held at Boroughbridge. Granted a charter by Charles I in 1622, it was a famous fair for cattle, sheep and horses – as indicated by the street named Horsefair. Special lemon curd tarts were also baked and sold, called 'Barnaby tarts'.

The second Friday in June was also the occasion for the annual Middleton Feast – or, as it was officially known, the Middleton Foresters Club Feast. They were another friendly society, and on their Club Day, as it was known, members would process around the village, dressed in green and holding a green stick, accompanied by banners and a brass band. They would then attend a church service before gathering for the main event – a large communal dinner, followed by music, activity stalls, and fairground attractions. This tradition was sadly ended by the Second World War.

12th

One traditional way of curing warts was to stick a new pin into an ash tree, then into the wart, then back into the tree. Within six weeks, it was believed, the wart would be gone.

13th*

First held in 1948, the Blessing of the Boats is an annual service at Whitby in which a vicar blesses the boats at the harbour and prays for God's favour on the fishermen. Traditionally held on Sea Sunday – the second Sunday in June – in recent years it has been associated with Lifeboat Day.

14th

A well at Brayton, near Selby, was known to be a pin well. R. C. Hope, in his 1893 collection *Holy Wells of England,* described one tale associated with it, as published in the *Leeds Mercury*. In the story, a young woman came to the well to drink the waters, which were believed by locals to aid in matters of love. There she had a vision in a dream of one of her lovers. The fairies, who wanted better arrows than the ones they were currently using, devised a method of gathering them; they said to the woman that if anyone wanted to find out the identity of their future husband, they must drop a pin into the well. They urged her to tell as many people as possible, and thus it became known as a pin well.

In another version, which dubiously claims the practice of pin-throwing to have existed for hundreds of years since the Medieval times, the Abbot of Selby Abbey attempted to put a stop to the pin-well by dedicating it to the Virgin Mary and re-naming it as 'Our Lady's Well'; however, this did little to stop the practice.

15th

It was common to use a stone with a natural hole through it, called a 'hagstone' or 'witch-stone', to ward off witches and bring good luck. In 1894 it was reported that, in Whitby, these stones were tied to front door keys to '"ensure prosperity to the house and its inmates.

16th

Jenny Greenteeth is a popular figure in folklore who is said to hide in lakes or ponds and lure children to their doom. With long green hair like underwater weeds and foul green skin, she probably originated as a means for parents to scare children away from potentially dangerous water.

17th*

The Walkington Hay Ride was an event which took place each year on the third Sunday in June, an occasion when dozens of colourful and richly decorated wagons and carriages were pulled through the streets by horses, their passengers all wearing Victorian costumes. Unfortunately, after forty years, the Hay Ride was cancelled, with the last held on this day in June 2007.

18th

Today marks the anniversary of the Battle of Waterloo in 1815, when a combined British and European army defeated Napoleon. There was much rejoicing back home, and in the small village of Denby Dale, near Huddersfield, the villagers decided to bake a pie. They had already made one in 1788 to celebrate the temporary recovery of George III from mental illness, but we have no record of when it was made or what its contents were. Shortly after Waterloo, though, we know that the villagers baked a large pie which contained two whole sheep, twenty fowl, and was served at a large communal feast. As you'll discover later on, this was just one of many in a tradition of huge pies coming out of Denby Dale.

According to Gerald of Wales, a bishop and historian who died in 1223, Osana was a saint who was buried and venerated at Howden, in East Yorkshire. Claimed to be the sister of King Osred of Northumbria – of which there were two in the eighth century – historians have found no record of her existence. Nevertheless, Gerald claimed that a priest's mistress who sat on Osana's tomb was miraculously stuck there and whipped until she repented. Her feast day was set as the 18th June.

19th

This song, titled 'The Pit Boy', was written during the nineteenth century and became very popular in mining areas after being published in response to the Warren Vale Colliery disaster in South Yorkshire in December 1851. Fifty-two men and boys had died after an explosion in the coal mine.

> The sun is sinking fast, mother, behind yon far blue hills,
> The signal bell has ceased, mother, the breeze of evening chills:
> They call me to the pit, mother, the nightly toil to share:
> One kiss before we part, mother, for danger lingers there.
>
> My father's voice I hear, mother, as o'er his grave I tread,
> He bade me cherish thee, mother, and share with thee, my bread,
> And when I see thee smile, mother, my labour light shall be:
> And should his fate be mine, mother, then heaven will comfort thee.
>
> Nay, dry thy tearful eye, mother, I must not see thee weep;
> The angels from on high, mother, o'er me their watch will keep.
> Then oh! Farewell awhile, mother, my fervent prayer shall be,
> Amidst those dangers dire, mother, that heaven may comfort thee.

Warren Vale Colliery, Rawmarsh, Rotherham.
© Fionn Taylor, CC BY-SA 2.0

20th

Whitby Museum lays claim to owning a mummified human hand, reputedly the only 'Hand of Glory' in existence. Discovered in the early twentieth century, it was buried in the wall of a cottage in Castleton. A Hand of Glory was allegedly the pickled right-hand of a criminal, cut off whilst the body was still hanging on the gallows and used by burglars to send the inhabitants of a house to sleep. One story holds that the hand was used to hold a candle made from human fat, whereas another claims that the fingers itself were lit. If one of the fingers didn't light, then it meant that someone in the house was still awake. This light, it was believed, could only be extinguished by blood or skimmed milk.

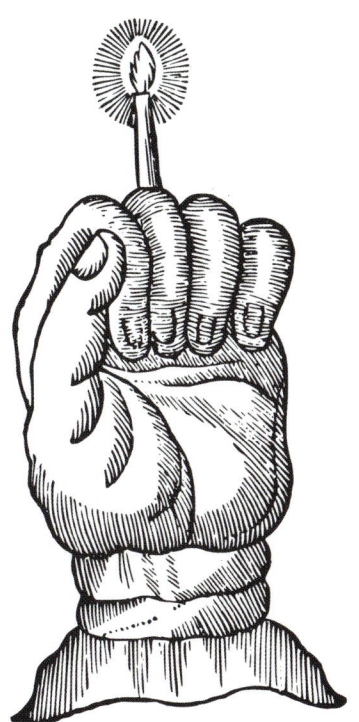

A 'Hand of Glory'.
Source: Wikimedia Commons

21st

Newburgh Priory is rumoured to be one of the possible burial sites of Oliver Cromwell. He died in 1658, and many places have laid claim to being the location of his body. Mary, his daughter, married into the family who owned the Priory, and from then on the legend took hold that she had secretly paid to have her father's body returned to her and buried somewhere in the Priory or grounds. Though no excavations have been conducted, one place in Yorkshire which definitely *does* own an element of Oliver Cromwell is Bolling Hall in Bradford, which contains a copy of his death mask.

Oliver Cromwell's death mask, at Bolling Hall, Bradford. Source: Catherine Warr

22nd*

The sheepdog – the ever-faithful companion to many a Yorkshire farmer – can compete in the annual Harden Moss Sheep Dog Trials, which sees some of the finest dogs in the country herd sheep competitively. A staple in the Yorkshire farming calendar, other attractions include various dog shows, sheep shearing and dry-stone walling demonstrations, and family activities. The trials are over a century old and are held each year in June.

23rd*

George Walker, in 1814, reported that it was customary for newcomers to a town or village in some parts of Yorkshire to set a meal outside their new home on the first Midsummer Eve after their arrival. Neighbours who wanted to make their acquaintance with the new family would then sit down and enjoy the meal with them.

The Dumb Cake ritual, which can be found on 20th January, could also be performed on Midsummer's Eve, as shown in this newspaper clipping from an 1870 issue of the *Leeds Mercury*:

> I shall never forget what I did last Midsummer-eve. I and my two sisters tried the dumb-cake together: you must know, two must make it, two bake it, two break it, and the third put it under each of their pillows, but you must not speak a word all the time, then you will dream of the man you are to have. This we did; and to be sure I did nothing all night but dream of Mr. Blossom. The same night, exactly at twelve o' clock, I sowed hemp-seed in our backyard, and said to myself: 'Hemp-seed I sow, hemp-seed I lies, and he that is my true love come after me and mow!' Will you believe me? I looked back and saw him behind me, as plain as eyes could see him.

Midsummer Eve, from George Walker's 1814 *The Costume of Yorkshire*. Source: NYPL Digital Collections

24th*

The Hepworth feast is held on the last Monday of June and commemorates the end of the 1665 Great Plague. There were many similar events held in surrounding towns and villages, however Hepworth's is the only one to survive. A procession, accompanied by a brass band, marches through the streets to the neighbouring village of Scholes and stops at points to sing hymns. At the village there are various stalls and entertainments, including a traditional roast pig.

A brass band plays at the Hepworth Feast. Source: Averil Shepherd

25th

Washing sheep, which gradually died out in the twentieth century, usually took place in late June. Thomas Joy recalled sheep washing at the Blea Beck on Grassington Moor:

> They started gathering at nine o'clock. The big fold held a thousand sheep, which were let through into the next and finally into the small catcher's fold. Each sheep was thrown in by two men standing on the bank, one at each side of the gate. They held onto the wool of the breast and buttocks and threw so that the sheep landed in the water on its back. The washers grabbed the animal by the forelegs, dollied [washed] it, particularly the belly and tail. As they swam across, the dirt floated out.

These occasions were often enjoyed by the whole family, with food, drinks, and even sports all part of the washing day experience.

26th*

First held in 1978, the Broughton Hall Game Show was a key event in the Craven social calendar, raising money for the Cave Rescue Organisation and the Upper Wharfedale Fell Rescue Association. As of 2012 it had raised around £325,000 for the two organisations, and one highlight of the show was The Birdman Challenge – a 40ft leap across a river, often in a variety of home-made costumes – with a £1,000 prize going to the winner. No one ever successfully completed the challenge. The show was sadly cancelled and last held on this day in 2011.

27th*

Thump Sunday is the name given to the Sunday after the feast of St John the Baptist (24th June) in Halifax. The name supposedly derives from the fact that you were allowed to thump anyone who went to the pub and didn't pay for his drink! It was the traditional end to a four-day fair which began the preceding Thursday, and which had, by the Victorian times, grown to become a considerable tourist attraction; it was estimated that 3,000 people alighted at Brighouse alone for it in 1859. Thump Sunday was also a day when people would set off for seaside holidays, with loud horns sounding at dawn to wake everyone up for the journey.

28th*

In the 1880s 'Wakes Weeks' were established to give industrial workers a holiday, and in Brighouse this became known as 'Rush Week'. Taking place on the Monday and Tuesday after Thump Sunday, it was officially adopted in 1908 and all the businesses in the district closed. However, this died out in the 1960s as workers were given more holiday time across the year and newer businesses did not follow the tradition.

29th

Though bear-baiting is an incredibly cruel and unfair form of entertainment by our modern standards, it was nevertheless a highly popular past-time in history. A misericord depicting it can be found at Beverley Minster. It fell out of popularity by the eighteenth century and was eventually banned in 1835, with the last (alleged) bear-baiting event held at The Dog Inn at Knottingley. Despite traditional bear-baiting being banned, it was still common in the Victorian times to keep bears in pits, where members of the public could torment them in their own way.

The misericord at Beverley Minster depicting bear baiting. Source: Beverley Minster PCC

30th

'There is a widespread belief,' wrote Rev. M. C. F. Morris in 1892, 'that if the cock crows in the house, or if the fowls enter it, visitors may be expected. I remember very well going to a farm house in Cleveland once, and being told by the farmer that they had been looking for a visitor because the cock had been crowing on the doorstead.'

July

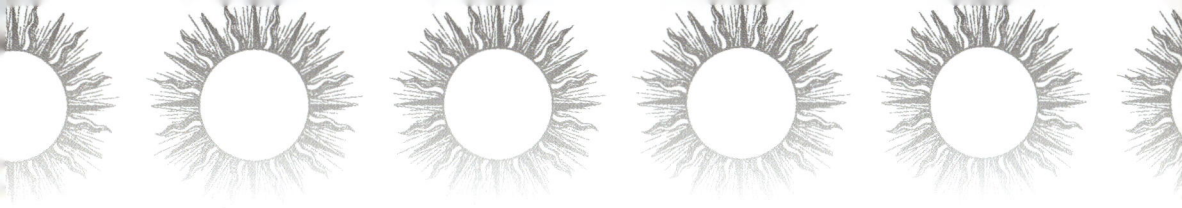

1st

Sheffield was once the scene of what could be described as ghost hysteria. In 1873 a number of sightings of a figure in white were reported in the city, and soon hundreds of people began travelling to see it. As reported in the *Sheffield Telegraph*:

> Not less than two thousand persons, principally youths and young men, congregated in the haunted district, much to the annoyance of residents. A numerous staff of police officers were there ready to receive them as soon as a large number got together. As might be expected the Ghost did not make his appearance, much to the chagrin of the assembled roughs.

However, as David Clarke writes in *Strange South Yorkshire*, this ghost became a long-lasting feature of Sheffield folklore and was still being talked about until the 1980s.

Interestingly, it seems that the 'ghost' soon morphed in popular imagination into the Victorian penny-dreadful staple Spring-Heeled Jack, with a later writer recalling that:

> Hundreds of people would congregate there at nights gazing expectantly at a yawning black hole underneath the Cholera Monument Grounds, the said hole being popularly supposed to communicate by way of an underground passage with the Manor Castle. Extra police were needed to keep the crowds in order, and if any juvenile was too inquisitive he was promptly and effectively dealt with by a policeman known far and wide as Owd Platts. These crowds talked of Spring-Heeled Jack who is even now shelved by the Penny Horribles …

One Victorian artist's interpretation of the popular folklore character Spring-Heeled Jack. Source: Wikimedia Commons

2nd*

One Yorkshirewoman in 1966 recalled that:

> Our village church had a feast day in July when the Sunday School scholars, followed by a large congregation, walked behind the huge banner with a picture of the Good Shepherd embroidered on it. The village brass band led us to different points in the village where hymns were sung. We always had a new frock for this, the biggest day in our calendar. Afterwards there was a tea in the Sunday School.

3rd*

Rev. M. C. F. Morris, in 1892, recorded this unusual custom:

> At Helmsley there is still held once a year what is called the Vardy Dinner. In the days before the Government appointed sanitary officers, Helmsley elected its own local committee to inspect the town once a year as regards sanitary matters. In the evening the inspectors met, supped, discussed, and gave their 'verdict'. Hence Vardy Dinner. The form, I am told, is still kept up, but chiefly for social purposes. The dinner is held annually, the committee having earlier in the day gone through the form of walking through the main streets, scrutinising at least the outside of dwellings as they pass. The Helmsley folk jokingly warn one another on this important day thus: 'Look to your drains and chimneys'.

However, it is unclear precisely at what time of year this took place or when it began to decline in practice.

4th

For many years the Zouche Chapel Well in York Minster – named after the fourteenth-century Archbishop William la Zouche – was well known as a

healing well. Water was drawn up from the well by a bucket, which remains there to this day, and the healing properties have been attributed to the mineral levels in the water absorbed from the limestone walls.

Zouche Chapel Well. Source: tuckdbpostcards.org

5th

Sheep clipping usually took place ten days after washing (25th June). Gilbert Brown, a Dales farmer, remembered that when he worked at Lamb Hill farm in Bowland they would shear a thousand sheep in a day. There would be eighty or ninety men (and many women) working, the latter providing snacks and a meal at the end. The farmer would send word round, and men came from four or five miles away to help with the shearing. They would work indoors, sitting on stools along both sides of a large barn as the sheep came down the middle. When shorn, the sheep would go out at the end and two men, who were waiting by the door, would dab tar onto any cuts the sheep had. The whole day would have an almost festival atmosphere as, after washing, the workers would have a hot meal with beer, then bring out instruments and start dancing. So important were clipping days in the social year that many would feel hurt if they were left out.

Tom Roberts' Shearing the Rams, 1890. Source: Wikimedia Commons

6th

The ducking stool was often used on those accused of witchcraft, as seen in this diary entry from 6th July 1699:

> Susan Ambler was whipped and put on ye Duckinge Stool for causing an evil spell on Adam Clarke's sheep, he only got two score lambs and nine were black ones, thys was at Stokesley.

7th*

The Oxenhope Straw Race is held on the first Sunday in July every year in Oxenhope, near Keighley. It started after a bet between two men over racing from one pub to the next whilst carrying a bale of straw, and it has since grown into a highly successful charity fundraising event, raising around £300,000 for good causes to date. Teams – often dressed in a variety of wacky costumes – must race around a two-and-a-half-mile long course, stopping at intervals to drink a pint. They will also be doused in water at certain points, and so the whole event makes for an entertaining day out.

Two creatively costumed participants at the Oxenhope Straw Race. Source: Averil Shepherd

Held on the Sunday after 6th July, the Kilburn Feast is a beloved local event. Here is how Marie Hartley and Ella Pontefract described it in 1946:

> Kilburn's feast and sports survive as an occasion in the year, not as a pathetic relic. The feast itself is set in the main street, and for weeks beforehand the children save up for the event. On the last evening the custom is kept up of electing a procession through the village. The Lord Mayor visits every house, criticizing something about it or the garden and demanding a fine. The Lady Mayoress, impersonated by a man, is allowed to kiss every lady 'she' meets that night.

Held in July each year, the Pontefract Liquorice Festival celebrates the rich heritage of liquorice in the town. Filled with stalls, entertainment, and history, the festival contains one of the widest ranges of readily available liquorice products and heritage information in the country.

The Liqourice Bush Pub at Pontefract. Source: Averil Shepherd

8th

Great worms or dragons are common in Yorkshire folklore, and one is said to have plagued the village of Sexhow. As recorded in 1888:

> Whence it came, or what was its origin, no one knew. So voracious was its appetite that it took the milk of nine cows daily to satisfy its cravings; but we have not heard that it required any other kind of food. When not sufficiently fed, the hissing noise it made alarmed all the country round about; and, worse than that, its breath was so strong as to be absolutely poisonous, and those who breathed it died. This state of things was unbearable, and the country was becoming rapidly depopulated. At length the monster's day of doom dawned. A knight, clad in complete armour, passed that way, whose name or country no one knew, and, after a hard fight, he slew the monster, and left it dead upon the hill, and then passed on his way. He came, he fought, he won; and then he went away. The inhabitants of the hamlet of Sexhow took the skin of the monster-worm and suspended it in the church, over the pew belonging to the hamlet of Sexhow, where it long remained a trophy of the knight's victory, and of their own deliverance from the terrible monster.

Whorl Hill, thought to be be home of the Worm of Sexhow. Source: Paul Buckingham/ Whorl Hill/ CCBY-SA 2.0

9th

One cure for whooping cough, collected in 1892, was to pass a child nine times over the back and under the belly of a donkey!

Image source: Shutterstock

10th

'Racing for the garter' was a common custom in which competitors raced for the honour of removing the garter – or bridal band – from a bride's leg. One account recalls that:

> Mistress Curtis was wed thys daye Juli ye 10th, 1687. To her garter band was founde stitched a goldien piece, on her bande was worked in fine silk these words, in two lines of smalle letters, with other enchantynge devices –

> 'Be thou as true to ye mayde round whose legge thou'llt bynde my garter,

> As I schalle always be to hym who bounde yt round my legge.'

11th

Summer is the breeding season for many seabirds, and this led to 'Climming', or egg collecting, at the cliffs of Bempton and Flamborough. Local men and women would gather at the cliffs and lower others down on ropes, collecting eggs as they went. It was an extremely dangerous activity which required a great deal of skill, trust, and bravery, as participants were often faced with a sheer and deadly drop into the sea. But despite the dangers, it was a highly popular community tradition, as whole families would get involved. It was banned in 1954 over concerns about declining bird numbers.

July 11: Boys Collecting Eggs on Cliff Face by James Clark Hook. Source: Wikimedia Commons

12th

This song is said to have been sung at the Kilburn feast (see 7th July) for over a hundred years. Like many folk songs, a large portion of the lyrics were made up as the singer went along, so this version is just one of hundreds of possible.

> Awd Grimy were a queer awd chap,
> 'E's deed, 'e'll dee no moor:
> 'E used to wear an awd frock cooat
> A-buttoned down afoor.
>
> *Chorus*
>
> Awd Grimy were a queer awd chap,
> 'E's deed, 'e'll dee no moor.
> Noo can ye sing another verse
> Diff'rent ti t' yan afoor?
>
> Awd Grimy bowt a load o' bricks
> To build 'is chimney higher,
> Ti keep 'is neighbours' cats an' dogs
> Frae slickin' out the fire.
>
> Awd Grimy 'ad a lahtle pig
> An' it were double jointed;
> 'E aimed to mackin' pork on it
> But 'e was disappointed.
>
> Why do these bugs torment me so?
> Ah nivver did 'em 'arm:
> The' come ti me when Ah'm asleep,
> Aye thousands in a swarm.
>
> There was a bug amang this lot,
> The' called 'im Great Big Joe;
> 'E 'ad two rows o' double teeth
> Upon 'is bottom jaw.

A squirrel is a funny bod,
'E wears a bushy tail;
Ya day 'e teeuk awd Grimy's coat
An' hung it on a rail.

Awd Grimy's great big bug was stuffed
An' put upon a shelf,
An' if ye want another verse
Ye can mack it up yerself.

13th*

Named after the Lyke Wake Dirge (June 4th), the Lyke Wake Walk is a 40-mile challenge walk across the highest and widest part of the North York Moors National Park. Created by Bill Cowley in *The Dalesman* in 1955, it was issued as a challenge to be completed in a 24-hour period. It was successfully completed shortly afterwards in 23 hours. The walk has developed its own club, whose members have created elaborate rituals, ceremonies, and hierarchies associated with it. It has been held as a race since 1964 on the Saturday nearest to the 10th of July.

Part of the Lyke Wake Walk. Source: James F Carter via Wikimedia Commons

14th*

Arguably the most famous show in Yorkshire is the Great Yorkshire Show, which runs from the second Tuesday in July until the following Thursday. Held at Harrogate, it is the largest agricultural show in England and attracts over 100,000 visitors each year. An early form was held in Fulford in 1838, but by 1843 it had become popularly known as the Great Yorkshire Show.

15th

The Seamer Fair, near Scarborough, is one of Yorkshire's oldest running fairs and a highlight in the Traveller calendar. A charter for the fair was granted by Richard II in the fourteenth century, making the fair one of the longest running in the county at around 600 years old. It is traditionally opened by the town crier proclaiming 'Oyez, oyez, oyez', at which point a representative, mounted on a horse, reads the charter at various points in the village. Permission was once given for any householder to open for the fair as an ale house if they displayed the branch of a tree above their door, and as many as twenty houses would brew their own beer and sell it at the fair! Recent centuries have seen the arrival of traditional Traveller wagons, which can still be seen to this day. Originally six days long, the fair has now sadly been reduced to running for only a single day. It takes place annually on the 15th of July.

16th

At the hamlet of Stape, in North Yorkshire, is a well named Old Wives' Well. It was a popular healing well, where visitors would wash the body part which needed healing with a rag dipped into the water. The rag would then be hung on a nearby bush, and as the rag rotted the body part was believed to heal.

17th

A humorous take on the 'race for the garter' custom can be found in the wedding of Mistress Bella Matthews, who was married approximately a week after Mistress Curtis (July 10th).

> Bella Matthews [...] mayde a ryghte cunninge device, for when she came to lift her skirt the kneeling winner founde her bande secure beyond removal, yt being helde fast about her legge by a smalle silve locke and hanging therefrom was smalle note ye whyche the bridegroom begged of the winner to remove, the whyche he having done, and finding that he could not decipher, offered to do the same. And these war ye words he read and whyche war alsoe cunningly worked on ye bande among leaves and many scrolls and other pleasing devices:
>
> 'Not thys alone but alle of mee
>
> Is locked, my husband holds the key.'
>
> At this the winner axed for the key, but ye bridegroom unlocked yt, lettigne ye winner tayke yt off, thereby saveing muche offence, yt was quite emblematickal and a pretty sight to witness, but yt would only doe for a bride to stand soe longe who was exceedingly well favoured in ye shape of her legges, but Mistress Bella knew the like could not be shown for miles around.
>
> I saye yt was a sight to witness.

18th*

The Topcliffe fair was a highly popular horse fair held every year in mid-July since 1343, until the royal charter was withdrawn in 1970. By the nineteenth century it had become one of the most important horse fairs in the North of England. A staple in the traveller calendar, as late as 1961 as many as seventy caravans were reported at the fair. However, concerns from local residents meant that 1969 was the last ever Topcliffe fair, making it one of the longest running fairs in the country.

An old gypsy caravan. Source: Wikimedia Commons

19th

This lover's lament, titled 'Sheffield Park', was first printed in around 1794 and has since become a popular folk song.

Down Sheffield Park a maid did dwell,
A brisk young man he loved her well,
He courted her from day to day,
At length he stole her heart away.

One morning upstairs to make her bed,
She lay down her weary head,
Her mistress came and to her did say,
'What is the matter with you today?'

'Oh, mistress, oh, mistress, you little do know,
What trials and troubles that I undergo.
Place your right hand upon my left breast,
My fainting heart it knows no rest.'

'Then write him a letter and write it with speed,
And send it to him if he can read,
And bring me an answer without delay,
For young Colin has stolen your heart away.'

'Then gather leaves to make my bed,
A feathery pillow for my weary head,
And the leaves they flutter from tree to lea
Will make a covering o'er me.'

There is a flower that bloometh in May,
That's seldom seen by night or by day,
And the leaves they flutter from tree to lea
Will make a covering o'er me.

20th

One of the most popular characters in Yorkshire folklore is Robin Hood. Though it is tempting to try and uncover the historical figure who may have inspired the character, it is important to realise that the Robin Hood we are familiar with is, like King Arthur, a largely mythical figure filtered through hundreds of years of literature, art, and folklore, and that any historical person who might have been the inspiration for them would be unrecognisable to the character that we know today.

One Robin Hood story with a direct link to Yorkshire is that of Robin Hood and the Pinder of Wakefield. Dating from the sixteenth century, the story involves a pinder – a man in charge of impounding stray animals – who claimed that none would dare to trespass in Wakefield whilst he was around. Robin, however, heard him, and when he and his men approached the pinder they were turned away and asked to leave. A fight soon broke out, and the pinder emerged victorious. Impressed by his fighting ability, Robin asked him to join his men. The pinder agreed, but only after Michaelmas.

21st

Green was widely regarded as a very unlucky colour for a bride to wear, and one old woman from a village near Whitby recalled to Rev. M. C. F. Morris that many young girls would rather have gone to church to be married in their common, everyday clothes than in a green dress. She insisted that one bride, who fell ill shortly after being married, had done so as punishment for wearing green on her wedding day.

22nd

On 19th May we read of the importance of informing bees of the death of a relative, but one Victorian writer recorded a much more elaborate ritual. Black cloth would be tied around the hives in mourning and, during the wake after the funeral, a small portion of food would be left for the bees; the belief was that if food was not left for them, they would die.

Telling the bees of the death of a family member.
Source: *The Century Illustrated Monthly Magazine*, vol. 18 (1879)

23rd

There are many beliefs and customs associated with death – such as opening the window to allow the soul of the departed to escape – but one unusual one was that a sick person could not die if they were laid on a bed made of wild bird feathers. Rev. M. C. F. Morris was told of a woman from Westerdale, near Scarborough, who was very ill for a week and resting on a bed of feathers. When she was moved off the bed, she died!

24th

Iron was believed to be able to deter witches, and naturally horseshoes – which were made of iron – soon became associated with this very purpose. William Henderson, in 1866, remembered a farmer telling him:

> How one of his horses had more than once been ridden by the witches, and he had found it in the morning bathed in sweat, but he had nailed a horseshoe over the stable door, and hung some broom over the rack, and the horse had not been used by the witches since.

25th

An unusual cure for thrush was recorded near Yarm. It was believed that if someone who was born after the death of their father blew three times down the throat of the one suffering from the disease, then they would be cured.

26th

The first visit of a newborn baby to another house was viewed with great importance. It was believed that the baby should be given three things: an egg, some salt, and white bread or cake. In East Yorkshire it was reported that they were given a few matches to light their way to heaven.

27th

One Victorian wedding custom was to throw a handful of coppers to children as the wedding party left the church. Rev. M. C. F. Morris claimed that it was also common at one time to fire a salute from guns filled with feathers, though it is difficult to establish how widespread this custom was.

28th

This story, collected by S. Baring-Gould from the original court documents in his collection of Yorkshire oddities, illustrates how prevalent beliefs about supernatural justice were in Yorkshire. There once stood, between Raskelfe and Easingwold, a lonely inn called The White House. There, in 1623, lived a man named Ralph Raynard who was romantically involved with a servant girl at Thornton Bridge. After an argument they parted ways and saw no more of each other. It was then that a man named Fletcher, who lived in Raskelfe, met the young servant and married her. However, it was not long before she had feelings for Ralph again. The girl (now Mrs Fletcher) began to be seen more and more at The White House, and her husband soon caught wind of the rumours that his wife was meeting her old lover. One day, he had to go to Easingwold on business and would not be returning until late. Feeling some premonition of evil, before he left, he sent a letter to his sister which read:

If I should be missing, or suddenly wanted be,

Mark Ralph Raynard, Mark Dunn, and mark my wife for me.

[Mark Dunn was Ralph's ostler].

As Fletcher was returning on foot from Easingwold, he was suddenly set upon by none other than Ralph and Mark! They threw him into the water and strangled him, and when he was dead and limp Mrs Fletcher helped place his body into a sack and drag it towards The White House. They buried the body in a recently disturbed area of the garden, and in the freshly dug soil – on top of the body – Ralph planted mustard seeds. People wondered what had become of Fletcher, but his widow's excuses were convincing enough to avoid suspicion. Ralph later rode to Topcliffe Fair (see 18th July). He stopped at an Inn, and as he stabled his horse he suddenly saw the ghost of Fletcher, 'pale, with a phosphoric light playing about him, pointing to him, and saying, 'O, Ralph, Ralph! Repent. Vengeance is at hand!' Ralph fled out of the stable, but soon recovered himself and shrugged it off as simply an hallucination. Browsing through the fair, he came to a jewellery stall and decided to buy a present for Mrs Fletcher. But again he saw the ghost – this time, wearing the same necklace that Ralph had picked out! 'How like you with a red streak round the neck such as this?' said the ghost. 'I will put one round the throat of my wife; and you shall wear one too!'

Ralph quickly rode off home, but could not escape the visions of the ghost. He saw it getting out of a sack, shaking and wringing water out of its clothes. It followed him as he galloped, leaving a luminous track on the road, and when Ralph reached The White House it faded into the ground where Fletcher had once been buried.

That night, Ralph's sister made him dinner. She placed before him a plate of mustard, and when Ralph looked up in shock he saw, sitting opposite him, the ghost of the dead man, pointing to his plate. Ralph sprang up and confessed everything to his sister. She ran off at once to the local sheriff, and all three – Ralph, Mrs Fletcher, and Mark – were arrested. They were hanged at York on 28th July, 1623. Their bodies swung in a gibbet on a hill by The White House, and after many years a rhyme emerged about Raskelfe – 'A wooden church, a wooden steeple, rascally church, and rascally people.'

29th

One wedding custom from East Yorkshire, as recorded by William Henderson in 1879, was that when a bride arrived at her father's house a plate of cake was thrown from an upper window onto the crowd below. The more pieces it broke into the better, because if it reached the ground unbroken it was a very bad omen for the marriage.

30th

One method of finding out the identity of your future lover was to find the first egg of a chicken and boil or toast it. You must then stand on something you have never trodden on before, take the egg, and cut it into portions. Then, in strict silence, eat it – shell and all – and walk backwards to bed. This, it was believed, would enable you to dream of your future partner.

Domestic poultry. Source: Wikimedia Commons

31st*

The Bradford Whit Walk was once one of the most popular competitive walking races in the country. The oldest amateur distance walk race in the world, it was held every Bank Holiday Monday and consisted of a 31-mile circular route around the Bradford area. The winner received the Hammond Cup, named after one of the Bradford businessmen who founded the walk in 1903. It was a hugely popular sporting event which was often used as training for British Olympic athletes. It was sadly cancelled due to dwindling numbers and last held on this day in 2011.

The Bradford Whit Walk. Image taken by Geoff Dowling

1st

The fiftieth anniversary of the repeal of the Corn Laws might not seem to us to be a particularly special occasion, but at Denby Dale it was considered important enough to warrant baking a pie for. The Corn Laws, originally designed to protect British farmers by preventing the import of foreign grains, ultimately led to high food prices and a considerable hunger amongst the poor. As such, when the Corn Laws were repealed in 1846, Denby Dale decided to bake a pie to celebrate (see 29th August). The anniversary pie, baked in 1896, contained:

- 1,120 lbs of beef
- 180 lbs of veal
- 112 lbs of mutton
- 60 lbs of lamb
- 20 stone of flour
- 24 lbs of lard
- 24 lbs of butter
- 30 lbs of suet

Taking over six hours to cook, when the pie was finished it weighed over a ton.

The Denby Dale Pie.
Source: foodsofengland.co.uk

2nd

Threshfield, in Craven, was said to attract pilgrims from far and wide to the Holy Lady Healing Well. The waters there were well known for healing ailments, and when Dulcie Lewis visited the well in 2001 for her book on Yorkshire cures, a mug had been chained to the well for those wishing to drink the water.

'St. Wilfrid', guided by a 'monk', processes through the streets of Ripon. Source: Averil Shepherd

3rd*

In Ripon a procession is held on the Saturday before the first Monday in August to re-enact the entry of St Wilfrid into the city. A seventh-century saint who was Abbot of Ripon and Bishop of York, Wilfrid was an important figure in the early Christian church in England and founded what is now Ripon Cathedral. The procession involves 'St Wilfrid', riding on a white horse, being led by a 'monk' and followed by a band to the cathedral, where he is then greeted by the Dean. There is usually a market held at the same time, and special tarts – known as 'Wilfra tarts' – are eaten.

4th

Ella Pontefract and Marie Hartley, writing in the 1940s, recorded a wedding custom apparent in the dales:

> We once met a girl in London whose grandmother rode to her wedding at Muker church on a white horse, on which she and the bridegroom rode back together after the ceremony, a custom in the dale in those days.

5th

Another story about Robin Hood is that of The Noble Fisherman, believed to date from the seventeenth century. As the story goes, one day Robin grew tired of hunting in the forest and decided to go to Scarborough to become a fisherman. He was hired by a woman with a boat, but was such a bad fisherman that he was laughed at by the crew and the woman. However, as they were out at sea, French pirates tried to storm the ship but Robin managed to shoot them all. Finding a huge pile of treasure aboard the French ship, he offered to split it with the rest of the crew on the fishing boat, but they insisted that he kept it.

6th*

The first Tuesday in August sees the annual gooseberry growing competition in the village of Egton. Competitive gooseberry growing was immensely popular in the eighteenth and nineteenth centuries across the country – so popular, in fact, that it even had its own national publication, *The Gooseberry Growers Register*! By 1845, there were 171 gooseberry growing shows in the country, but the hobby soon declined and the Register ceased publication in 1916. Today, only the Egton show and a handful of shows around Cheshire remain. It is believed that the first show to be held at Egton was in 1800.

7th

First performed in 1911, a 'Josh Wedding' was held in order to raise money to cover medical costs for injured miners. Participants would dress up as bride, groom, guests, and relatives of the couple and hold a mock wedding, often with comical costumes. The tradition began to decline after the introduction of the NHS, but was revived at Lotherton Hall in 2018.

8th

The Stocksbridge Bypass Ghost, in Sheffield, illustrates how folklore evolves and develops in a community. In 1987, a number of people began reporting ghost sightings and experiences around the Stocksbridge bypass. Since then, it has become known locally as 'the Ghost Bridge' and entered popular lists of haunted sites, where those seeking their own experiences can visit.

9th

Bolling Hall, in Bradford, is said to be the scene of a famous haunting. In 1643, during the Civil War, the town came under siege from the Royalists. The Bolling family were sympathetic to the Royalist cause and allowed the Royalist commander William Savile to stay with them. As the story goes, he was so angered by Bradford's Parliamentarian sympathies that he ordered his soldiers to kill anyone they could find the next day. That night, Savile was visited in the chamber where he stayed by a ghost, who told him to 'pity poor Bradford.' Shaken, Savile withdrew his order from the previous day and Bradford was taken with little bloodshed. The earliest version of this story dates from 1776, and so it is unclear as to whether Savile really did see a ghost.

The room at Bolling Hall where William Cavendish is said to have seen a ghost whilst staying there in 1643. Source: Catherine Warr

10th*

The Whitby Regatta, held every year in August for over 170 years, is one of the oldest regattas in the country and a major tourist attraction for the seaside town. What started off as a competition between local fishermen soon grew into a popular yacht racing and rowing event, attracting 20,000 people each year. Though yacht racing declined and is no longer held at the regatta, competitive rowing is still a major attraction.

11th

The 'Yorkshire motto' is very famous, but few are aware that at one time it was part of a song. Norman Creaser, who was born in 1919 and spent his life as a farmer, wrote down this song which he'd learnt growing up:

My ord father he used ti say ti me,
'Here's a bit o' summat that Ah'll 'a ti tell ti thee,
Thoo knows nowt, tha's nobbut very dense,
Thi 'eead is full o' summat but it isn't full o' sense.
Ah's gan ti give thee a bit o' good advice,
No need ti tak offence becos it's nowt but common sense.
Thoo mun 'ear all and thoo mun know nowt,
And thoo mun see all and thoo mun say nowt,
And thoo mun tak all an' thoo mun gi' nowt,
And thoo mun sup all and thoo mun pay nowt,
An' if ivver thoo does anythin' fer nothin' allus do it for thissen

12th

Known as the 'Glorious Twelfth', this is the traditional start of the grouse shooting season. A staple of the agricultural calendar, the Yorkshire moors are home to some of the biggest and most popular grouse shoots. The red grouse, one of the most highly prized birds, can only be found in the red moorland of the UK.

13th

Believed to be the oldest chartered fair still in existence, Lee Gap Fair – held at West Ardsley, near Leeds – was granted to Nostell Priory by Henry I in 1135. It traditionally ran twice a year for three days, from the 13th to the 15th of August and from the 6th to the 8th of September. It was named after Thomas Leigh, a commissioner sent by Henry VIII to value Nostell Priory and its lands. There is a stained-glass window in St Mary's church at Woodkirk which shows a scene of the fair and a brass plate which reads:

> It [Lee Gap fair] was reckoned amongst the most famous in the country, and to which it is said merchants from France, Spain, and even Germany came to sell their merchandise. During the time of the fair, the priest and clerk stood ready all day, to marry all such as were desirous to enter the matrimonial state. Miracle plays were performed at the fair, the object to bring religion home in a tangible form to the frequenters.

14th

Children born on Sundays were believed to be protected from evil spirits. William Henderson, in 1879, recalled being told by a woman that those born during the hour after midnight had the ability to see the spirits of the dead.

15th

Scarborough Fair is famous nowadays as a folk song, but it was once a huge, 45-day long event which started on the 15th of August each year and ended on the 29th of September. It was extremely unusual for fairs to last this long, and so Scarborough Fair was quite remarkable. The charter was granted in 1253, and the fair attracted merchants from all over Europe and from as far afield as the Ottoman Empire. The fair finally came to an end in 1788, but has cemented a lasting legacy through the popular folk song.

Gillis Mostaert, *Village Feast*, 1590. Source: Wikimedia Commons

16th

One type of wood which was believed to hold anti-witch properties – like rowan wood – was 'wicken wood'. Though difficult to establish precisely which tree it came from, the power of the belief in this 'wicken wood' was attested to by Rev. M. C. F. Morris' 1892 account of a discussion he had with an old woman:

> I said to her, 'Can you tell me what they call the tree from which they get the wicken-wood?' 'Naw,' she said, 'Ah's seear ah can't, bud ah knaw 'at wicken-wood 's t' stuff 'at they mak whip-stocks on for witches.' I professed surprise that they should do such a thing now or at any time, and added that at all events I supposed she had never heard of any case where the fact of the whip-stock having been made of wicken wood had been of the slightest use for the supposed object. 'Aa, bud ah ev,' she replied; and went on to say that a witch used to hant (haunt) a certain 'brig' which she named. 'Did anything ever happen at the brig?' I enquired. 'Happen! aye; an' ah 'll tell ya an' all.' 'I should like to know what it was,' I said. 'Whya then,' she continued, 'Yah day (it wer a good bit sen noo) sum lads was cumin' wi carts, an' as seean as ivver they com near-hand t' brig t' fo'st draught was stopped; t' lads leeak'd, bud they couldn't see nowt; then they shooted on him ti gan on, an' he tell'd 'em 'at he couldn't: t' hosses couldn't storr; all was stopped.' To the best of my recollection there were four or five carts altogether, when some impassable barrier seemed to stop the way over the bridge. But my old friend continued her story by saying, 'Noo, yan o' t' lads had gitten a wicken-wood whip-stock; an' when he com up he said he would try; an' then summat leyke spak ti t' draughts, "here 's t' lad cumin' wit' wicken-tree gad"; an' away they went; sha (the witch) couldn't stop 'em then.' Such was the story of the power of the wicken-tree whip-stock almost verbatim as it was told me, and not a shadow of a doubt did my informant seem to have of the literal truth of it.

17th*

Whitby Folk Week, which was first held in 1965, has since grown into one of the largest and most popular folk festivals in Britain. Celebrating the folk music, stories, and dancing of the British Isles, it features over a hundred artists and performers in a variety of locations across Whitby. It is perhaps one of the best opportunities to witness traditional Yorkshire folk music and storytelling, and his held annually in August.

18th

Published in *The Annals of Wakefield House of Correction* in 1904, this song was recorded as the 'Rothwell Debtors' Prison Song', sung at a Debtor's prison near Leeds.

> We bid you welcome, brother debtor, to this poor but nary place,
> Where no bailiff, bum or satyr dare to show his frightful face.
>
> Now, kind sir, as you're a stranger down your garnish you must lay,
> Or your coat will be in danger, you must either strip or pay.
>
> Ne'er repine at your confinement, from your childer and your wife,
> For wisdom lies in true resignment, through the varied scenes of life.
>
> What was it made great Alexander weep at his unhappy fate?
> It was because he could not wander through this wide, strong prison gate.
>
> Every island is a prison strongly guarded by the sea.
> Kings and princes for that reason prisoners are as well as we.

19th

An extract from the *Settle Chronicle*, dated 1854, tells us that:

> Some twenty years ago the 19th August was a day of great importance to the Curriers, Dealers and Shoemakers of this District. The neighbourhood of the Talbot Inn [Now the Talbot Arms in Settle] was crowded with the sons of Crispin and the sellers of Leather, and numerous traders in 'Sparables' from that once great Shoe-nail mart, Silsden. It was no uncommon thing to see empty Leather waggons standing in the streets and Inn yards, whilst the bulky bundles of 'Bend' were offered for sale in the Barns and Sheds of the Inn yard. Dealers and Shoemakers came from fifty to sixty miles round. This year the only relic of this once great Leather Fair were a couple of Silsden nailers.

One of the reasons for the decline of this was the emergence of a leather fair in Leeds in 1827, which drew away much of the business.

20th

One unusual remedy for warts was recorded in 1892. On the night of a new moon, someone must go outside and observe where the moon was in the sky, then bring the afflicted outside. They then had to rub their warts with soil without looking at the moon, then return to the house. The warts, it was believed, would then be cured.

Image source: Shutterstock

21st*

Brighouse, like many places in Yorkshire, practised rush-bearing. A four-day event, it started on the first Saturday after the second Thursday in August and involved maypoles, dancing, and a great deal of drinking – which makes it remarkably similar to the rush-bearing events held at Sewerby Bridge and Saddleworth (see 6th of September and 24th of August respectively). It is generally believed that rush-bearing originated as a means of ceremonially removing the used rushes from the floors of churches, however, what makes the Brighouse custom interesting is that rush-bearing was held there *before* a church was built. Similarly, in neighbouring villages like Rastrick and Lightcliffe, where churches *did* exist, there are no records of the custom taking place. It may be that the people of Brighouse adopted the custom from other villages as an excuse to have a party! Rush-bearing appears to have died out by the mid-eighteenth century and was replaced by a fair, but it was revived briefly in 1865. Unfortunately, this revival did not persist and the custom swiftly died out again.

22nd

Hazelnuts and their trees were sometimes called 'filberts', probably because they ripen around the time of this day, St Philbert's day. Hazelnut trees were often prized for their flexible shoots, known as withes or writhing wands, which could be cut and bound together and used for building or crafts.

Hazelnuts.
Source: Racool,
Freepik

23rd*

Late August sees the arrival of the Halifax Fun Fair, and though nowadays it is just a typical fair, it inherits a legacy of spectacular entertainment. In previous years the fair included Parish's Temple of Thespis, 'which had a lofty proscenium arch with classical columns and pediment, an apron stage and open auditorium'. Marie Hartley and Joan Ingilby recorded the typical amusements which could be found at an early twentieth-century fun fair in Yorkshire:

> Helter skelters, Shamrock and Columbine swing boats, roundabouts, cake walks, coconut shies, hoop-la and brandysnap stalls, pie and pea stalls with monkeys running up and down poles, and the bursts of gay music and the dazzling lights of the steam organs.

Swing boats.
Source: Wikimedia Commons

24th*

The second weekend after 12th August sees the annual Rush-bearing festival at Saddleworth, originally in West Yorkshire but now part of Greater Manchester. In this festival, rush-carts – sometimes standing up to 16ft high and with a rider straddling atop – are dragged through the streets by hand and converge on the parish church of St Chad at Uppermill. The procession stops outside many pubs en route, and at each pub a kettle – which holds five pints – is filled up with beer and hauled up by the rider to the top of the cart, and there they are expected to drain it. To be chosen as rider is considered a high honour, requiring an ability to keep a cool head, maintain balance, and have a high tolerance for alcohol.

Rush Bearing at Long Millgate by Alexander Wilson, 1821. Though this is in Manchester, it is very similar to the rushbearing at Saddleworth, which was historically in the West Riding of Yorkshire. Source: Wikimedia Commons

In previous centuries the festival often saw much more violence than it does today. When two carts came face to face, with no room to pass, fists were often used as a means of determining right of way. In fact, the whole festival seems to have been treasured as an opportunity to have a fight – Ella Pontefract and Marie Hartley, in their *Yorkshire Tour*, recall the story of a father asking his son if he had been in a fight. When the son replied that he hadn't, the father told him to get on with it and then they could go home! Riders could also be killed if the cart ran aground.

By the end of the nineteenth century the custom had almost completely died out, until it was revived in 1975. An old lady recalled the tale that if a barren woman touched the rush-cart, she would become pregnant within a year – which lends credence to the theory that the festival was influenced by male fertility rituals.

The village of West Witton in Wensleydale is famous for the 'Burning of the Bartle'. Held on the Saturday closest to the 24th of August – the feast of St Bartholomew – villagers create a hideous effigy of 'Bartle' and parade him around the village. They recite a poem:

The Burning of the Bartle.
Source: Averil Shepherd

On Penhill Crags he tore his rags
Hunters Thorn he blew his horn
Cappelbank Stee happened a misfortune and brak' his knee
Grassgill Beck he brak' his neck
Wadhams End he couldn't fend
Grassgill End we'll mak' his end
Shout, lads, shout!

To which the crowd responds with a 'hooray!' After the procession, Bartle is taken to an area where he is stabbed, covered in fuel, and set on fire.

The Burnsall Fell Race, which is held every year in August, is reputed to be the oldest race of its kind in Britain, with local legend holding that it has been held since Elizabethan times. With a steep climb and precipitous descent, it has become immensely popular as a local sporting event.

25th*

Every Bank Holiday Weekend sees the West Indian Carnival descend on Leeds. One of the oldest running carnivals in Europe, it was first held in 1967 and drew around a thousand people. Today, it sees an estimated 150,000 people enjoy an explosion of colour, floats, and celebrations of heritage and culture over the weekend.

A fantastically dressed participant at the Leeds Carnival.
Source: Wikimedia Commons

26th*

Held every year at the end of the first-class cricket season – around late August or early September – is the Scarborough Cricket Festival. Started in 1876, it consists of a series of matches with the Yorkshire County Cricket Club and has grown to become a popular event. With a relaxed, holiday feel around the ground, it makes for an exceptional summer day out.

27th

To celebrate the Golden Jubilee of Queen Victoria in 1887, the villagers of Denby Dale decided to bake a pie. The ingredients included:

1581 lbs of beef
180 lbs of mutton
163 lbs of veal
180 lbs of lamb
250 lbs of lean pork
64 rabbits
3 hares
42 fowls
40 pigeons
12 grouse
21 ducks
4 plovers [a type of small bird]
1 turkey
5 geese
2 wild ducks
108 small birds
40 potatoes

Once all the ingredients were in the pie, it weighed nearly 1 ½ tons. On the day of the pie cutting, thousands of people gathered to watch. However, when the first cut was made, the crowd instantly recoiled – it had turned bad! Such was the stench of the pie that many ran away, and it is said that the hounds of a local hunt smelled it from five miles away and came over to investigate. Despite the horrendous smell, many people actually tried to get hold of the pie and for over an hour fought and scrabbled over scraps. The next day, the remains of the spoilt pie were taken away in solemn procession and buried in quicklime.

28th

The possibility of baking a huge pie to celebrate the end of the First World War had occurred to many at Denby Dale, but due to a shortage of materials the idea was abandoned. However, an opportunity to bake a large pie emerged when it was discovered that the Huddersfield Royal Infirmary was in need of funds to improve its medical services. Hence, in 1928, Denby Dale decided to bake its biggest ever pie to raise funds. It was so big that a new baking dish had to be made, measuring 16 ft by 5 ft and standing 15 inches tall. It weighed over a ton and had to be placed in a specially built oven. The pie included:

600 lbs of beef

15 hundredweight of potatoes

2 hundredweight of lard

80 stone of flour

2 stone of baking powder

This resulted in 100 cubic feet of pie, which was enough to serve 40,000 people! Commemorative plates were even made, and the event raised £2,000 (around £126,500 in today's money) for the hospital and other local causes.

29th*

In 1846 the Corn Laws were repealed by Prime Minister Robert Peel (see 1st August). When these laws were repealed, the people of Denby Dale decided to celebrate by baking another huge pie. This pie contained:

44 ½ stone of flour
91 ½ lbs of suet
191 lbs of lard
161 lbs of butter
100 lbs of beef
11 lbs of pepper
1 calf
5 sheep
7 hares
14 rabbits
4 pheasants
4 partridges
2 brace grouse
6 pigeons
2 turkeys
2 guinea fowls
4 ducks
4 geese
4 fowls
63 small birds

Measuring 21 ft in circumference and 1 ft 10" deep, it took 10 ½ hours to bake and, when finished, was led onto a temporary stage in a field by a farmer's wagon. Speeches were made, and the number of people standing on the stage increased until – in the middle of one speech – the stage collapsed! Joseph Peace, who was to have the honour of formally cutting the pie, reportedly fell inside it. Suddenly the crowd – which numbered around 15,000 people – surged forward, scrambling madly in a riot until both the stage and the pie were utterly destroyed.

Held on this day on alternate years is an unusual method of election known simply as the 'Kirby Hill Races'. It was used to choose two wardens for the hospital of St John the Baptist, an almshouse founded in 1556, whose founder laid down the elaborate rules of election. The rules are as follows:

> The vicar and two churchwardens each produce a key with which to open the Dakyn chest, in use since 1784. A water-filled stone urn, known somewhat prosaically as The Pot, is removed from the chest and carried ceremoniously to the adjoining schoolroom.
>
> The Pot holds the names, written on waterproof paper and encased in wax, of the four unsuccessful candidates at the last wardens' election. The Waxman, aforesaid, breaks the seal, reads the names and discards them. The Waxman seals another six names – chosen from 'the gravest and most honest' – in hollowed pieces of candle and places them in The Pot. The vicar stirs the pot, averts his gaze and picks from the six nominees the names of two new wardens. The Pot with the remaining four names are again locked in the chest, only to be opened in the event of what now would be called a byelection.

The trust which the creator of this ritual founded is still ongoing and is believed to be the oldest of its kind in Europe; it provides grants for students and flats for the elderly.

Another unusual event which happens this time of year is the Septennial Boundary Riding. Taking place every seven years – most recently in 2018 – it dates from the time when Richmond was given a Royal Charter by Elizabeth I in 1576. The mayor, as Lord of the Manor – accompanied by his councillors, officers, and townspeople – must 'beat the bounds' of the town. This involves walking around the boundary of the town – approximately 15 miles – often stopping at points for a proclamation to be read declaring this area to be the 'ancient and undoubted boundary'. At two points along the route the Mayor is carried over the River Swale on the back of the Waterwader, and at five points along the route the Mayor throws freshly minted pennies to children. One member of the entourage carries a special axe for the removal of any obstruction to the progress of the Riding. Perhaps one of Yorkshire's most bizarre traditions, it is well-loved by the local community and often draws huge crowds.

30th

Margaret Clitherow, who was born in York and executed for her Catholic faith in 1586, has some interesting folklore connected to her hand. Her final burial place remains unknown, and though there are some suggested locations – such as beneath the alter of St Saviour's church in Stydd – there is no proof as to any location. Wherever she was buried, one legend posits that her body was secretly taken away by Catholics who cut off her right hand as a relic. This right hand, which at one time was alleged to be seen in The Old Black Swan in York, soon turned up in the Bar Convent. Though not proven to be the hand of Margaret Clitherow, it is widely believed to be so, and healing miracles have been attributed to it. Her feast day is today.

31st

In Yorkshire, it was often believed that baptism could heal sicknesses. William Henderson, writing in 1879, records that:

> "The infant child of a chimney-sweeper at Throne, in the West Riding of Yorkshire, was in a very weak state of health, and appeared to be pining away. A neighbour looked in, and inquired if the child had been baptised. On an answer being given in the negative she gravely said, 'I would try having it christened'. The counsel was taken, and I believe with success."

September

1st

The period from September to October was when the last of the harvest was taken in, and to celebrate this a 'churn' or 'kern' supper was held by the farmer for his workers. The name derives from the churn of cream which was often circulated around the feast. From the mid-nineteenth century, however, practices like this began to fall out of use as harvest festivals held in the parish church became more popular. Up until the end of the 1870s, churn suppers often saw the 'burning of the old witch', where eight or ten small heaps of peas, on dry straw, were gathered together and set on fire in the field. The workers then ran and danced about, eating the peas and blackening each other's faces with the burnt straw. One churn supper song can be found on 4th September.

2nd

Legends about disturbed burial grounds are extremely common, and Yorkshire has its own fair share. At Stannington, in Sheffield, are the remains of a Quaker burial ground, now known as Bowcroft Cemetery. As David Clarke describes in *Strange South Yorkshire*:

> A blasphemous farmer living in the nearby wild uplands decided that tombstones from the burial ground would be more useful in his cellars and on his farm than 'hiding the clay of such as these'. So one night he carted all the tombstones away. The spirits of the tombs haunted him and his household forever afterwards.

3rd

A week after the disastrous Corn Laws pie (29th August), the villagers of Denby Dale tried to rescue their dignity by baking another, named the Resurrection Pie. This time, however, there was no publicity or visitors – just a large pie with which the villagers could celebrate the end of the Corn Laws. It was placed on a cart and distributed among the village.

This day in 1988 also saw the creation of the Bicentenary Pie, celebrating 200 years since the first pie was made in Denby Dale (see 15th June). Containing 3,000 kgs of beef, 3,000 kgs of potatoes and 700kgs of onions, it entered the Guinness Book of Records as the biggest meat and potato pie in the world. With a BBC Radio One live broadcast to celebrate, in two days 90,000 people were served a slice of pie.

A Denby Dale pie dish. Source: Etsy.com

4th

In Holroyd's *Collection of Yorkshire Ballads*, published in 1892, is the 'Craven Churn-Supper Song'. It comes with the following note attached:

> At these churn-suppers the masters and their families attend the entertainment, and share in the general mirth. The men mask themselves, and dress in a grotesque manner, and are allowed the privilege of playing harmless practical jokes on their employers, &c. The churn-supper song varies in different dales, but the following used to be the most popular version. In the third verse there seems to be an allusion to the clergyman's taking tythe in kind, on which occasions he is generally accompanied by two or three men, and the parish clerk. The song has never before been printed.

> God rest you, merry gentlemen!
> Be not moved at my strain,
> For nothing study shall my brain,
> But for to make you laugh:
> For I came here to this feast,
> For to laugh, carouse, and jest,
> And welcome shall be every guest,
> To take his cup and quaff.
>
> *Chorus.*
>
> Be frolicsome, every one,
> Melancholy none;
> Drink about!
> See it out,
> And then we'll all go home,
> And then we'll all go home!

This ale it is a gallant thing,
It cheers the spirits of a king;
It makes a dumb man strive to sing,
Aye, and a beggar play!
A cripple that is lame and halt,
And scarce a mile a day can walk,
When he feels the juice of malt,
Will throw his crutch away.

'Twill make the parson forget his men, –
'Twill make his clerk forget his pen;
'Twill turn a tailor's giddy brain,
And make him break his wand,
The blacksmith loves it as his life, –
It makes the tinkler bang his wife, –
Aye, and the butcher seek his knife
When he has it in his hand!

So now to conclude, my merry boys, all,
Let's with strong liquor take a fall,
Although the weakest goes to the wall,
The best is but a play!
For water it concludes in noise,
Good ale will cheer our hearts, brave boys;
Then put it round with a cheerful voice,
We meet not every day.

5th

In 1963, there was a fear in Denby Dale that the tradition of making large pies was dying out. A public meeting was called to explore the possibility of making another one. The packed meeting voted overwhelmingly in favour of doing so, although at the time there was no specific event or anniversary in mind as the occasion. Initially proposed to raise funds for a village hall, there soon emerged a more glamorous reason: in 1964 there were to be no fewer than four Royal babies!

This became the perfect excuse for a pie, and it was soon publicised on a scale never before seen. The pie dish – measuring 18 ft by 6 ft and 1 ½ ft deep – was actually used as a boat which was floated down the Mirfield canal. The pie itself included:

3 tons of beef

1 ½ tons of potatoes

½ ton of gravy and seasoning

½ ton of flour

¼ ton of lard

With 650 square feet of crust, on the day of its grand unveiling it was pulled by a traction engine as part of a half-mile long carnival procession through the richly decorated streets. Upon reaching the field, it was met with a huge fair and a crowd of eager spectators. 30,000 portions of pie were served up to the crowd.

6th

The first weekend in September sees the annual rush-cart festival in Sowerby Bridge (see 27th August). In this local variation, fortunately the rider on top of the rush-cart is not required to drink a kettle of beer. Instead, they must lower a large wooden triangle – which represents three local parishes and is placed on top of the rush-cart – as it passes under low bridges.

A rushcart at the Sewerby Bridge Rushbearing Festival. Source: Wikimedia Commons

7th

William Henderson, writing in 1879, recorded a superstition in East Yorkshire:

> Another death-omen is the crowing of a cock at dead of night. A lady in the East Riding of Yorkshire tells me that a few years ago, a cook, who had recently come to her from the north of that county, told her one morning, with tears in her eyes, that she should not be able to stay long in her place, for her sister was dead or dying. The mistress naturally concluded that the tidings had come by post that morning, but it turned out that such was not the case. The cock had crowed at midnight on two following nights, and as she had not heard from her sister for some time she was doubtless ill, if not already dead. Happily the good woman's fears were groundless, and she lived some time in my informant's service.

8th*

Hardraw Force, in the Yorkshire Dales, is England's highest single drop waterfall and the backdrop to Britain's second oldest outdoor brass band competition, held every year on the second Sunday of September. First held in 1881, it was revived in 1989 and has featured many of Britain's most popular brass bands.

Hardraw Force. Source: Wikimedia Commons

9th

This diary entry gives us just one of the ways in which Yorkshire folk sought to protect themselves from evil:

> On Friday night, September ye 9th, 1757, Robert George Tinbull, of Marske, was spelled on ye bridge ower an hour by Hester dale, the old witch of Marrick. His horse would not move until Tom Wilson came along with a wicken [rowan] staff. Then they both saw Aister run ower the road as a black cat. They both ken'd it was her, for she hath meant him harm for a good spell. But the bridge is haunted.

The rowan tree has for a long time been associated with warding off evil, and so it is not surprising that Tom Wilson had a staff made out of one!

10th

One of the most famous Yorkshire ghost sightings is that of a legion of Roman soldiers marching underneath Treasurer's House in York. They were seen by a young engineer who was working in the cellars of Treasurer's House and saw 'about twenty soldiers walking two abreast [...] carrying lances, round shields and short swords'. Many initially dismissed his story because he recalled them carrying round shields, when it was believed that they only carried square shields; however, later research has shown that in the fourth century AD, soldiers equipped with round shields were stationed in York. Further credence was lent to the story when archaeological research revealed that a Roman road does actually run underneath the cellars of Treasurer's House.

Rowan.
Source: Shutterstock

11th

There are many stories involving knights and dragons in Yorkshire, and this poem from 1685 – 'The Dragon of Wantley' – satirises many of their common features, including the use of spiked armour, a key element in the popular tale of the Lambton Worm and the dragon of Loschy Wood (17th May). The original version contains nineteen verses, so for the sake of brevity I have shortened it to thirteen.

Old stories tell how Hercules
A dragon slew at Lerna,
With seven heads, and fourteen eyes,
To see and well discern-a:
But he had a club, this dragon to drub,
Or he had ne'er done it, I warrant ye:
But More of More-Hall, with nothing at all,
He slew the dragon of Wantley.

This dragon he had two furious wings,
Each one upon each shoulder;
With a sting of his tayl, as long as a flayl,
Which made him bolder and bolder.
He had long claws, and in his jaws
Four and forty teeth of iron;
With a hide as tough as any buff,
Which did him round environ.

In Yorkshire, near fair Rotherham,
The place I know it well,
Some two or three miles, or there-abouts,
I vow I cannot tell;
But there is a hedge, just on the hill edge,
And Matthew's house hard by it;
O there and then was this dragon's den,
You could not chuse but spy it.

George Bickham's eighteenth-century illustration of The Dragon of Wantley.
Source: Wikimedia Commons

Hard by a furious knight there dwelt,
Of whom all towns did ring,
For he could wrestle, play at quarter-staff, kick, cuff and huff,
Call son of a whore, do any king of thing,
By the tail and the main, with his hands twain,
He swung a horse till he was dead;
And that which is stranger, he for very anger
Eat him all up but his head.

These children, as I told, being eat [by the dragon],
Men, women, girls, and boys,
Sighing and sobbing, came to his lodging,
And made a hideous noise;
'O save us all, More of More-hall,
Thou peerless knight of these woods;
Do but slay this dragon, who won't leave us a rag on,
We'll give thee all our goods.'

'Tut, tut,' quoth he, 'no goods I want:
But I want, I want, in sooth,
A fair maid of sixteen, that's brisk and keen,
With smiles about the mouth,
Hair black as sloe, skin white as snow,
With blushes her cheeks adorning,
To anoynt me o'er night, ere I go to fight,
And to dress me in the morning.'

This being done, he did engage
To hew the dragon down;
But first he went, new armour to
Bespeak at Sheffield town,
With spikes all about, not within but without,
Of steel so sharp and strong,
Both behind and before, arms, legs, and all o'er,
Some five or six inches long.

To see this fight, all people then
Got up on trees and houses;
On churches some, and chimneys too;
But these put on their trowses,
Not to spoil their hose. As soon as he rose,
To make him strong and mighty,
He drank by the tale six pots of ale,
And a quart of aqua-vitae.

Our politick knight, on the other side,
Crept out upon the brink,
And gave the dragon such a douse,
He knew not what to think:
'By cock,' quoth he, 'say you so, do you see?'
And then at him he let fly
With hand and with foot, and so they went to't;
And the word it was, Hey boys, hey!

'Your words,' quoth the dragon, 'I don't understand;'
Then to it they fell at all,
Like two wild boars so fierce, if I may
Compare great things with small.
Two days and a night, with this dragon did fight
Our champion on the ground;
Tho' their strength it was great, their skill it was neat,
They never had one wound.

At length the hard earth began to quake,
The dragon gave him a knock,
Which made him to reel, and straitway he thought,
To lift him as high as a rock,
And thence let him fall. But More of More-hall,
Like a valiant son of Mars,
As he came like a lout, so he turn'd him about,
And hit him a kick on the a…

'Oh,' quoth the dragon, with a deep sigh,
And turn'd six times together,
Sobbing and tearing, cursing and swearing
Out of his throat of leather;
'More of More-hall; O thou rascal!
Would I had seen thee never;
With the thing at thy foot, thou hast prick'd my a… gut,
And I'm quite undone for-ever.'

'Murder, murder,' the dragon cry'd,
'Alack, alack, for grief;
Had you but mist that place, you could
Have done me no mischief.'
Then his head he shaked, trembled and quaked,
And down he laid and cry'd;
First on one knee, then on back tumbled he,
So groan'd, kickt, s…, and dy'd.

12th

A short distance from the Birkdale Beck, a tributary of the River Swale, was an inscribed border stone known as Hollow Mill Cross which dated from the fifteenth century. According to local legend, in 1664 a stocking buyer named John Smith was returning to Kirkby Stephen when he was suddenly set upon and murdered. Local suspicion fell on a Westmorland farmer named James Hutchinson, but there was not enough evidence to convict him. Two years later, Hutchinson was returning home from a thunderstorm after attending a funeral in Muker, and saw the ghost of his victim. Startled, he was thrown from his horse, and died when he fell against the stone cross.

Hollow Mill Cross. Source © Roger Templeman (cc-by-sa/2.0)

13th

'Robin Hood and Guy of Gisborne' is widely regarded as being the most violent of Robin Hood stories, and certainly a marked difference from the rather sanitised image of Robin Hood we have today. It dates from the seventeenth century, and in the story, Robin dreamt that he was beaten by two yeomen who stole his bow. Upon waking, Robin vowed to find a yeoman and punish him, despite Little John reminding him that it was just a dream. Robin soon saw a yeoman in the forest, and he and Little John argued over whether they should send in some men before they went in themselves. As a result of the argument the two parted ways, and Little John returned to Barndale forest in South Yorkshire. However, when he arrived he found the Sheriff chasing after his men, and despite shooting one of the soldiers dead, he was captured and tied to a tree.

Meanwhile, Robin Hood encountered Sir Guy of Gisborne in a forest. Guy was lost and, not recognising Robin for who he was, asked him to guide him through the forest. On the way, Guy told Robin that he was searching for Robin Hood, and Robin, his true identity still a secret, challenged him to an archery contest. After Robin beat him in the contest, he asked Guy for his name, which he revealed. In return Guy asked Robin, who revealed his true identity. They soon fought, and when Robin tripped over a root Guy quickly wounded him in the side. Robin then prayed to the Virgin Mary for help, and afterwards managed to kill Guy. He then cut off his head and stuck it on to the end of his bow and, with a knife, mutilated Guy's face so that it was unrecognisable. After swapping clothes with Guy, he went to Barnsdale forest. There he rescued Little John, and the ballad ends with Little John killing the Sheriff of Nottingham with Sir Guy's own bow.

This illustration of Robin Hood fighting Guy of Gisborne, as seen in Henry Gillbert's 1912 *Robin Hood and the Men of the Greenwood*, conforms to our popular image of the folk character – but with less violence than the original story. Source: Wikimedia Commons

14th*

The St Leger Stakes in Doncaster, held annually in September, is the oldest of the five British Classics, widely regarded as the pinnacle of British flat horse racing. It was first raced in 1776, and not only is it older than the other four races, but it is also longer than them and the last to be run in the season.

St. Leger Stakes, Doncaster. Source: Wikimedia Commons

15th

A 'Mell supper' was a common tradition in which a large meal was served to celebrate the last of the harvest being gathered, rather like the churn supper on 1st September. The 'Mell' was the last sheaf of corn to be gathered, and the proceedings of a Mell supper were recorded by Rev. M. C. F. Morris in 1892:

> No mell supper can take place without dancing, and formerly the advent of 'guisers' formed one of the great features of the entertainment. These 'guisers' were men with masks or blackened faces, and they were decked out in all sorts of fantastic costumes. The starting of the dancing was not always an easy matter, but by degrees, as the dancers warmed to the work and as the ale horns came to be passed round, the excitement began to grow; this was increased by the arrival of the 'guisers', and then the clatter of the dancers' boots doing double-shuffle and various comical figures, set the entertainment going at full swing. The 'guisers' would at times come uninvited to the feast, and as a rule they were well received, but sometimes the doors would be barred against them and their entrance stoutly resisted. About fifty years ago it was very common when the 'shearing' of the corn was finished for three large sheaves to be bound together; for these, races were run by the women amid the greatest excitement. This also was called the mell sheaf, and would contain about a bushel of corn, and in the days when wheat was at such a high price as it once was the prize was worth having.
>
> I have been informed that at Kilburn, on the Hambleton Hills, the mell sheaf was tastefully made of various kinds of corn plaited together and covered with ribbons, flowers, &c. When the guests were ready for the dance, the mell sheaf would be placed in the middle of the room, which was frequently a disused one, and they danced round it. It was made like a figure and was sometimes called the mell doll.

16th

One of the most famous folklore figures from Yorkshire is Mother Shipton. Believed to have been born in 1488 in Knaresborough, her life is one which has been continually mythologised by writers hundreds of years after her death. She was believed to have been a popular local herbalist, providing home cures and remedies for the people of Knaresborough, but later gained the power of prophecy. The earliest collection of her prophecies was published in 1641, eighty years after her death, and many others were fabricated by later writers. Her petrifying well in Knaresborough – which can give objects left there a stony exterior due to natural processes – has become a highly popular tourist attraction.

Mother Shipton's prophecies – many of which turned out to be later forgeries – quickly gained popularity. Source: Wellcome Collection

17th

It was believed unlucky to leave the house if both the front and back door were open. It was also believed unlucky if the first person you saw on your journey was a woman. I. Hinton, a miner from Rotherham, recalled in the 1970s that if a miner on his way to work saw a woman on his journey, he would turn around and go back home!

18th

A final tale of Robin Hood is that of his death. In the ballad, Robin went to his cousin, a prioress, to be bled in order to cure some ailment. The prioress, however, deliberately let out too much blood and killed him. In other versions, it is her lover – Sir Roger of Doncaster – who killed Robin, by stabbing him in revenge for Robin having inherited Sir Roger's land and title. However, before he died, he managed to mortally wound Sir Roger. Little John vowed to that he would avenge Robin, but Robin forbade it, as he had never harmed a woman. In some later versions, Robin shot one last arrow and asked to be buried where it fell.

19th

Wheat is usually sown in the autumn, and Rev. M. C. F. Morris recorded that in the mid-nineteenth century, planting-time would also sometimes be accompanied by a festival:

> At the backend, when the early sowing had been completed, the farmer made a sort of feast for his men, the principal feature of which was a 'seed-cake', which was given to each of them. The cake did not get its name from anything that it contained, for it was in fact an ordinary sort of currant or plum cake, but from the occasion. On these minor festivals the men had as much ale to drink as they liked, and right well they enjoyed themselves. This old custom has, I believe, now quite died out.

20th

It was believed that a hob – a small household creature, such as the famous one at Farndale (25th February) – lived in a cave at Runswick Bay, near Scarborough. This hob was able to cure whooping cough and other ailments, and mothers would take their children there and call out for it to heal them or walk along the beach with their sick children.

21st

Held on the first Sunday and Monday after the 19th of September is the annual Redmire feast. Here is an account of the event in a 1948 issue of *The Dalesman*:

> At Feast time every house was filled with visitors and the population was at least doubled. The butcher who came round weekly with his trap always brought two traps at Feast weekend. A gay gathering of caravans, roundabouts, and stalls would crowd the Redmire Green, and there would be enthusiastic contests at quoits, 'wallops', and foot-races, with several trotting matches during the three days. There was, of course, a dance every evening. Local inns put up every sort of attraction they could in the way of singers, dancers and comedians, and did a wonderful business. […] The cheese-cake gathering was the highlight of the Feast. I think this came to an end about 1910, and I think I saw, and heard, the last. I was in the pastures about half a mile above Redmire when I heard so much noise that I thought the place had gone mad. I was told it was the cheese-cake gatherers setting out. Anyone and everyone joined in, so long as they were dressed in an absurd rig-out and – for preference – had blackened their faces. The whole body went in procession through the village. One or two would call at each house, often on the pretence of oiling the clock, and they would only come away when they had been given something to put in their baskets they carried with them. When they whole village had been visited the procession moved back to the local inn where the cheese-cakes were eaten.

22nd

It was widely believed that adding dark stout to baked goods, and stout in general, would help recovery from illness. This recipe is for a 'Yorkshire Get-Well Cake', and calls for a healthy dose of Guinness.

Ingredients

- 450g sifted flour
- 450g brown sugar
- 450g raisins
- 1 teaspoon of bicarbonate of soda, melted in a ¼ pint of Guinness stout
- 4 eggs
- 225g butter or margarine
- 113g glace cherries
- 113g mixed peel
- Grated rind and juice of a lemon
- Pinch of mixed spice

Method

- Rub butter into flour, and add other dry ingredients
- Beat eggs with the stout and bi-carbonate and blend well into mixture
- Turn into lined greased large tin, cover with greaseproof paper and bake in slow medium oven for 4 to 4 ½ hours, removing paper for last half hour. Cool in the tin.

23rd*

The Nidderdale show, known locally as the Pately show, is held in Pateley Bridge in September each year. First held in 1895, it is an important event which showcases some of the finest agricultural animals, produce, crafts, and helps keep local traditions alive. Regularly attracting tens of thousands of visitors, it marks the traditional end of the agricultural show season.

Nidderdale show ground.
Source: Wikimedia Commons

24th

Today is the feast day of Robert of Knaresborough, a hermit who lived in a cave by the River Nidd. Born in York in around 1160, he lived in various caves and hermit-holes (including under a church wall at Spofforth) and was well known for his charitable acts and reports of miracles. It is said that he was visited by King John and many others who sought physical healing, and pilgrims came from near and far to be healed by the medicinal oil which supposedly flowed from his tomb, cut from the rocky crags where he lived. Though never officially canonised, he is still regarded as a saint and churches are dedicated to him at Knaresborough and Harrogate.

25th

This is the anniversary of the Battle of Stamford Bridge, near York, when the English army of Harold Godwinson repelled the Norwegian army of Harold Hardrada and Godwinson's brother Tostig in 1066. There is the famous story that a single Norwegian, armed with an axe, managed to hold the bridge by himself and kill 40 Englishmen before he was finally slain by an English soldier floating under the bridge and stabbing him with a spear. To commemorate this event, each year at Stamford Bridge special oval-shaped pies are baked – with a skewer sticking out from the top, naturally.

26th

On 17th January was a story of blood being drawn from a witch, but this belief can actually be attested to in historical records. Margaret Morton, in 1650, was charged with bewitching an infant. The mother of the child stated that she pricked the witch with a pin, at which point the child immediately recovered. The accused 'witch' was tried but acquitted.

27th

Rev. M. C. F. Morris recorded the remarkable lengths which people would go to in order to protect their children against disease. A small village near Whitby had suffered an outbreak of measles, and one farmer, eager to protect his two children, knew of a traditional method of staving off the illness. He needed a donkey, however, but none could be found in the village, and so he took his family and walked four miles to the next village to get one. Going to the beach with the newly-acquired donkey, each child was placed on the donkey with their face towards the tail. Three hairs were then drawn from the tail, put into a bag, and tied around the child's neck. The donkey was then made to walk a certain distance on the sands nine times, all whilst a thistle was held over the child's head. Upon returning to their native village – in which few families had escaped from measles – the family were left unaffected by the illness and their belief in the power of this traditional remedy strengthened.

28th

William Henderson, writing in 1879, recorded that:

> In the West Riding of Yorkshire there is a strong feeling against burying a woman with her rings or jewellery. A gentleman told me that when his mother died he was desirous of leaving on her hand her wedding-ring, but was reproved for the wish by the women who laid her out. 'Ye mun no send her to God wi' her trinkets about her,' they said.

29th

S. Baring-Gould recorded the following Yorkshire superstition:

> It is said in that county that the first child baptised in a new font is sure to die [...] When I was incumbent of Dalton a new church was built. A blacksmith in the village had seven daughters, after which a son was born, and he came to me a few days before the consecration of the new church to ask me to baptize his boy in the old temporary church and font. 'Why, Joseph,' said I, 'if you will only wait till Thursday the boy can be baptized in the new font on the opening of the new church.' 'Thank you, Sir,' said the blacksmith, with a wriggle, 'but you see it's a lad, and we shu'd be sorry if he were to dee; na if t'had been a lass instead, why then you were welcome, for 'twouldn't ha' mattered a ha'penny. Lasses are ower mony and lads ower few wi' us.'

30th

Not just a trendy health spa town, Harrogate also experienced a healing-waters boom. A popular spa bath was established in the village of Lockwood, and by 1859 it had 30,000 visitors in one year. The *Yorkshire Gazette* described some of the benefits in 1834, as well as a new-fangled process recently arrived from India:

> At these baths, near Huddersfield, the Indian mode of shampooing, which found so delightfully refreshing, – those rather painful in its first operations, – is introduced; and as the water is well adapted to relieve persons suffering under debility, cutaneous disorders, rheumatism, &c., we have no doubt, but this pleasant and romantic retirement will become a fashionable place of resort during the summer months.

The site continued to operate as a public bath until 1941, when it was used as a gas storage depot.

Lockwood Spa. Source: Kirklees Images Archive

October

1st

A large horn can be seen inside The Rose & Crown Hotel in Bainbridge, North Yorkshire. Though no longer continued, the custom was to blow it each night from Michaelmas Eve (28th September) to Shrove Tuesday, to guide travellers who were lost on the moors.

The horn, formerly blown each night to guide travellers, now hangs in The Rose and Crown in Bainbridge. Source: Averil Shepherd

2nd

Easby Moor was said to be the location of a 'Devil's Court', where witches would gather together and plot. The site was actually the location of a Bronze Age settlement, complete with walls, pits, flints, and barrows. One of these barrows was named Nanny Howe, after a famous witch who lived in the area. The Victorian folklorist Richard Blakeborough reported that:

> Old people of Great Ayton still aver that on a certain night a once noted witch, Nanny Howe, may be seen riding astride on a broomstick over Howe Wood just at midnight. This witch, so mounted, is said once to have chased the devil for miles – on this occasion the two must have fallen out; perhaps at that time honest folk got their due. Howe Wood is near Kildale.

3rd*

A 'Court Leet' was a manorial court which played an important role in the early justice system. Its power was limited only to the lands of the Lord of the Manor, and the Court at Spaunton is one of only a few still active today. Meeting on the first Thursday in October, the Court is responsible for handing out fines for minor offences such as surfacing driveways and placing signs on the common. A traditional lunch of hare pie and Christmas pudding then follows.

4th

In the village of Harden, near Bradford, is St Antony's Well. It now appears to have run dry, but it may have contributed to a local tradition in the neighbouring town of Bingley. St Antony is the patron saint of swineherds, and in Bingley it was customary to bake 'Parkin pigs' which were eaten at autumn fairs in October.

5th

Molly Milburn, Percy Shaw Jeffrey tells us in 1923, was a famous witch in the village of Danby. However, as shown by this diary entry, she was often made the scapegoat for unfortunate events:

> Oct. ye 5, 1663. Molly Milburn was thys daye whipped for that she, been a witch, dyd worke great evil among Thos. Turner's cattel, soe that a grevious scab dyd brek out sorely among yem at ye same tyme.

6th

Whipping was a common punishment for those accused of witchcraft. As can be seen throughout this book, most of the accusations were based on claims of evil spells against people and animals, scapegoating those unfortunate enough to have been suspected as a witch:

> Aunt Eliza went to see Sebina Warters whipped in Leyburn and then made to walk along the Shawle [sic] in her shift, and to walk next daye same like but not to bee whipped, she having cast an evil spell on Robert Walker's dowter and brindle cow, so that both were milk bound and ye cow and bairn were like to die.

7th

For the first time in over 20 years, an unusual graduation ceremony was performed on this day in 2021 at Theakston's Brewery in Masham. Known as 'trussing in', the apprentice cooper (barrel maker) was placed into a 45-gallon cask, covered in used hops, rolled around, and then ceremonially sacked before being re-instated as a fully qualified cooper. Theakston's is one of only two breweries in the UK to still produce barrels.

8th

Rev. M. C. F. Morris, writing in 1892, recorded an unusual cure for whooping cough:

> Catch a frog, and put it into a jug of water; make the patient cough into the jug; this smits the frog, and the patient is cured. 'Did it do any good?' was asked in a certain case. 'Yes,' was the answer, 'the frog took it, and coughed as natteral as a Christian.'

9th*

For many years, Wibsey Horse Fair in Bradford was regarded by some as the largest horse fair in the country. Believed to have been started in the twelfth or thirteenth century by monks from Kirkstall Abbey, it grew into a beloved local tradition, with horses and ponies paraded through the streets and sold each October. It steadily declined in the latter half of the twentieth century, and after stopping entirely in the 1970s it was resurrected as a fun fair in 2010.

10th

Paulinus of York, whose feast day is today, was a monk from Rome who was sent to Britain in the seventh century by Pope Gregory I to convert the local populace to Christianity. Particularly associated with Northumbria, he became one of the most important figures in the early British church. He is said to have baptised thousands of people in the River Swale, which was dubbed by later writers as 'England's River Jordan'.

Facing page: St. Paulinus baptising King Edwin of Northumbria at York in 627. The site of the baptism, specially built for the occasion, would later become York Minster. Source: Wellcome Collection

PAULINUS baptizing EDWIN, the first Christian King of Northumberland, at York.

11th*

The Hull Fair is one of the longest-running and most popular traditions in the city. Held on the Friday nearest to 11th October and lasting for over a week, the oldest charter dates from 1278, meaning it has been running continuously in various forms for over 700 years. One of the largest travelling funfairs in Europe, it has featured a number of thrilling and unusual attractions over the years, including Birch's International Water Circus, in which £100 was offered to anyone who could swim across a tank of water whilst eating four sweets!

Hull Fair. Source: Wikimedia Commons

12th

'For a sore throat,' recalled Mrs Addy, 'Grandma, who lived in Huddersfield, would boil potatoes, mash them, and wrap them in a little cloth. The cloth was put into one of her stockings and then olive or camphorated oil rubbed onto the outside of the stocking. Then wrap the stocking round the neck until morning. It was a soggy lump in the morning but the sore throat had gone.'

13th

Belief in fairies (and the possibility of encountering them) was common in Yorkshire, as seen in this diary entry from 1650:

> Very earlie in ye morning Ralph Blackburn, George Pickersgill, Anthony Thompson and Mary his wife, having to go to Whitby when they came nigh unto Anthony Barker's small close they one and all espied many fairies disporting themselves righte merrilie in their sprightlie midnight revels. They watched yem for some time, until one dancing a little space from ye ringe discovered yem when, giving a signal, they departed on the instant, and not one of them kennd wither. Alle ye witnesses are of good report. Thys pleaseth ye Townsfolk mightily, none been syn Dan Outhwaite war murdered eight year cum Candlemas. Ye fairies were oft seen after thys, even by mysen as late as a week ago, T. R. [Thomas Rogers, who transcribed the notes from the original manuscript in 1695].

14th

In Richmond is the legend of Potter Thompson. As the story goes, one day he found his way into a cave in the rock below Richmond Castle. There he saw the sleeping King Arthur and his knights, surrounded by treasure – including the sword of Excalibur. However, when he tried to remove the treasures, Arthur and the knights awoke. Potter fled the cave in terror, but when he returned later, there was no trace of the cave.

15th

'The Barnsley Anthem' can trace its origins back to a 1911 songbook, and has since become a popular folk song in the area.

We're all dahn in t' cellar-'oil where muck slarts on t' winders,
We've used all us coil up and we're reight dahn to t' cinders;
If bum-bailiff comes 'e'll never finnd us,
Cos we're all dahn in t' cellar-'oil where muck slarts on t' winders.

We're all dahn in t' cellar-'oil where muck slarts on t' winders,
Door-'oil's wide oppen as it's oft bin afooer;
Fire-'oil it's nearly reight chock full o' cinders,
An t' wife she's aht callin' wi' t' neighbour next dooer,
Cos we're all dahn in t' cellar-'oil where muck slarts on t' winders.

We're all dahn in t' cellar-'oil where muck slarts on t' winders,
Door-'oil's blocked up wi' ashes an' cinders;
When t' chap comes for t' rent, will 'e be able to finnd us?
Ma comes wi' t' rollin' pin, Pa wi' t' berlinders,
When we're all dahn in t' cellar-'oil where muck slarts on t' winders.

Cheapside, Barnsley. Source: Wikimedia Commons

16th

An extract from a diary, dated 1695, tells us one of the ways people in Castleton, North Yorkshire, sought to shame and humiliate women who were pregnant out of wedlock – though in this case with unexpected results:

> By order of ye parsonne and Squire, Susie Markham and Polly Smallwell were browten publickly to church seated back side first on an ass apiece to shame them and do penance for that being withe child, but what amazement was brought about unto alle when that they were axed to declare who had led them into such a sadde plight. Susie rave the sheet from off her and spake so that alle might heare, 'Your sonne parsonne'. Then Polly dyd likewise and made speech saying, 'And I have been browte to this disgrays for that I dyd hearken to yet evil promises of Master Tom, ye squire's sonne. God forgive them and ye for that he have browhten us here.' The lasses were found to have spoken ye trewth but not untyl ye younge gentlemen war putten to ye oath. So they [the two women] stood not agen and my yonge gentlemen be gone I knowe not whither.

Castleton, North Yorkshire. Source: Wikimedia Commons

17th*

Yarm Fair, one of the oldest fairs in Britain, runs for three days in October each year. One of the main outlets for cheese selling, an 1822 Yorkshire Directory claimed that there was once 500 tons of it sold! A popular fair in the Traveller calendar, though the horse sales for which it was once famous have largely died out, it is still common to see horses parade and gallop up and down the High Street.

Caravans at the Yarm Fair. Source: Averil Shepherd

18th

Today is St Luke's Day, and it was once customary on this day to whip stray dogs on the streets. There was even a church official called a 'Dog Whipper', whose job was to keep stray dogs out of churches. Thankfully, with the advent of animal protection laws and dog shelters, this custom has died out.

19th

Though the superstitions shown so far in this book may be viewed by us today as the odd beliefs of people long ago, we must remember that they often had serious consequences. One very common belief in Yorkshire was that people could cast evil wishes on others, and in 1674 it led to this tragic event:

> Tommy Sutcliffe hanged hysel in Howe Wood, throw an evil wish, and was buried at ye four crossroads on ye moor and staked. Geo. Wilson, Amos Hunter, Geo. Scott, and Robert Armthwaite carried him thither, Thos. Scott drave the stake.

20th

There are many cures for warts in this book, and this one, recorded in 1892, is perhaps one of the strangest:

> A common black slug is caught and rubbed several times over the wart. The slug is then fixed tightly to a thorn on a hedge or elsewhere, and then left to die and wither away. It is supposed that simultaneously with this withering away of the creature the wart will also consume away and disappear. Only it is essential that the patient shall not again look at the slug, otherwise the healing power would be arrested in its operation.

21st

Today is the feast day of St John of Bridlington, also known as John Twenge, who was the last English saint to be canonised before the Reformation. Born in Thwing in 1320, there are a number of miracles associated with him – including turning water into wine and rescuing seamen from a shipwreck by appearing to them in the storm. One time he was struck by a large falling stone but suffered no harm, and such was his fervour during prayer that steam rose from his head. He was credited with restoring sight, mending broken limbs, and curing the plague. He died in 1379 and was canonised in 1401. Though associated mostly with women in labour and fishermen, Henry V reportedly prayed to him for victory at Agincourt, and the victorious outcome of the battle only solidified John's legend and powers.

St John of Bridlington.
Source: Wikimedia Commons

22nd

There have been many Yorkshire societies throughout history, but a surprising number of them have been based in London. The first meeting of the 'Gentlemen and others in and near London who were born within the County of York' took place in 1678, and in 1812 another Yorkshire society had established a school for boys and girls in London. In 1891 the Society of Yorkshiremen in London was founded. It flourished in the 1920s and '30s, and boasted of King George V and the then-Duke of York as patrons. The current Yorkshire Society, which is based in Yorkshire, was founded in 1980 and is dedicated to charitable works.

23rd

Black cats were seen as a seriously bad omen, as shown by this diary entry:

> Saw three black cats last night so did not go to market to-day fearing some evil, but it turned out well as Betty was taken with spasms and might have died had I not stayed at home and she is the best milker of all I have, this omen for ill brought naught but good.

24th

October and November saw the practice of 'salving' sheep. A farmer would smear the skin of a sheep all over with a mixture of oils, fats, grease and tar to kill parasites and prevent scab. The process was long and tiring, as each sheep would take around an hour to salve, and it was said that you could always tell when a farmer was salving because his hands were jet black for weeks on end. When dipping (using a liquid insecticide) became mandatory in 1905, salving eventually died out.

25th

Marie Hartley and Joan Ingilby, who recorded life and tradition in West Yorkshire, noted the ingenious methods which young children would use to keep themselves warm in the cold winter:

> Boys warmed their fingers on home-made hand-warmers, old cocoa tins with holes pierced with a nail at either end, filled at Hunslet with oily waste begged from railway engine drivers, or at Gomersal with cotton-band, round woven band used on spinning machines, which like the waste smouldered when lit. The cotton-band, called slow or wheely-band, was wrapped in paper by youths to make foul tasting cigarettes.

26th

William Henderson, in 1879, recorded a spell used by a woman in Wakefield to make her betrothed visit her:

> She obtained the blade-bone of a shoulder of mutton, and into its thinnest part drove a new penknife; then she went secretly into the garden, and buried knife and bone together, firmly believing that so long as they were in the ground her betrothed would be in a state of uneasiness, which would gradually increase till he would be compelled to visit her.

27th

One of the most common creatures in folklore is that of a black dog. Called a padfoot or a guytrash in Yorkshire, it was commonly described as having shaggy hair and eyes like saucers. Branwell Brontë, brother of the famous Brontë sisters from Haworth, described the guytrash which haunted the area around his home as 'a black dog dragging a chain'. Popular descriptions of the guytrash are similar to that of the barghest, as found on 28th February.

28th

Today is the feast day of St Simon the Zealot, one of Jesus' disciples, and one local legend held that the area around the village of Coverham was actually his burial place. The chapel, bridge, and well in the area are dedicated to him, and though we may dismiss this legend as simple fantasy, it is likely based on early legends which stated that he travelled to Roman Britain and preached there. However, Catholic tradition also holds that he was martyred in the Middle East, and so his true fate is unknown.

St Simon the Zealot. Source: Wikimedia Commons

29th

A popular folktale is that of the Upsall Gold. As the story goes, there was once a poor man who lived at Upsall, in Hambleton. For three consecutive nights he dreamt that if he stood on London Bridge he would hear something good. Believing this to be a sign, he decided to set off for London immediately. When he finally reached London Bridge, he waited and waited but nothing happened. At last, thinking he was probably a bit silly, he decided to walk home again. But just then he bumped into a stranger and the two began talking. They got onto the subject of the Yorkshireman's dream, at which point the stranger revealed that he, too, had had a strange dream; he had dreamt that he found a crock of gold under an elder bush in the castle yard at Upsall (there are the ruined remains of a large building or castle at Upsall, which belonged to the Scrope family). However, the stranger did not know where Upsall was. The Yorkshireman, feeling no need to enlighten the stranger as to the location, set off for Upsall to dig up the treasure for himself. He dug at the spot the stranger described, and lo and behold! There were multiple crocks of gold. And so he dug up a hoard of gold which made him rich for the rest of his days.

30th

A harrow-tooth is one of the sharp hooks on a harrow tool which breaks up the soil, and it appears to have been used in some home remedies. William Henderson recorded the following event:

> Some years ago, a relation of mine was crossing the moors from Whitby to his home at Stokesley, when he heard a woman's voice calling out loudly, 'Canny man, canny man, d'ye come frae Stousley?' On his replying that he did, she begged him to take a harrow-tooth to the wise man of that place, as her husband had been injured by it, and she wished the wise man to polish and charm it. He took the harrow-tooth and placed it in his pocket, but, truth to tell, as soon as she was out of sight, he flung it away among the heather. However, when, some time after, he passed that way again, the poor woman recognised him and thanked him heartily for doing her errand, saying that her husband had mended from the day the wise man got the bit of iron.

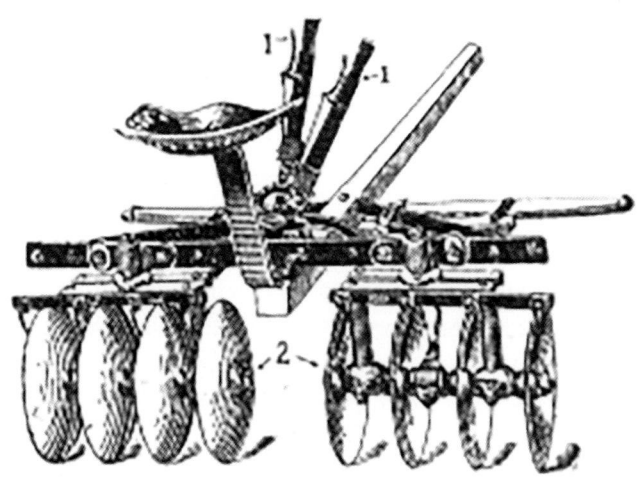

A disc harrow. Source: Wikimedia Commons

31st

Though today is known as Hallowe'en, in earlier years it was sometimes referred to as 'Mischief Night', as children would play pranks similar to those found on the more popular Mischief Night on 4th November. Also called 'nutty-crack night', Peter Brears records a custom in which young couples would try to divine their future happiness together by throwing pairs of nuts onto the fire; if they burnt quietly, it was a sign of successful marriage, but if they bounced and flew apart then the marriage was doomed to fail.

Today is also the feast day of St Begu, a Yorkshire nun who lived at the Hackness nunnery, near Scarborough, which had been founded by St Hilda of Whitby (see 17th November). Begu's claim to fame is that of supposedly witnessing the soul of St Hilda being carried to heaven by angels when she died in 680 AD, before news of her death had reached the nunnery. Begu died in 690, and in the twelfth century her remains were transferred to Whitby, where miracles were soon reported.

November

1st

Around November time it was common to kill the family pig, who had spent the year being fattened with household waste. It was customary (after the pig had been killed) to give some of the meat to neighbours, but the plate was not to be washed before being returned, as this was considered unlucky. Rather, it must be returned as used, or 'fully blodded'. It was also unlucky for a pregnant woman to help out in the curing of the pig meat. Parties and games often followed the pig-killing and it was said that every part of the pig was used – except for the squeak. Killing the pig in this manner was still being performed in the 1950s.

2nd

The feast of All Soul's Day was the occasion for making 'saumas loaves', a type of square cake or loaf containing dried fruit, similar to the soul cakes which were made all over the country. People would also go 'souling', which is similar to modern day trick or treating, in which they would dress up and ask neighbours for saumas loaves or soul cakes.

Soul cakes.
Source: Wikimedia Commons

3rd

A few miles west of Richmond stand three stones on a cliff which overlook Swaledale. These were erected in commemoration of Robert Willance, a prosperous Richmond draper who would often take to riding his horse over the moors alone, whatever the weather.

One day in November, as the story goes, a thick mist enveloped him whilst on the moors and forced him to return home. The details of the story change, but what is consistent with each one is that he leapt from the edge of Whitcliffe Scar and fell 212ft but miraculously survived, albeit with injuries. To give thanks for his incredible survival, he erected a stone at the place of his leap.

4th

Mischief Night, as it was known, was a popular time to play pranks. Dulcie Lewis records that:

> These [pranks] could be tapping at windows, ringing doorbells and running away, daubing door handles with treacle and removing gates. The privy was not a good place to linger on 4th of November. Little boys would open the door and throw a penny banger in, or if there were two privies side by side, tie together the two 'snecks' or door latches, leaving the occupants imprisoned.

Mischief Night also took place on 31st October in some parts, but in Yorkshire it was by far most popular on 4th November.

5th

Parkin is a common treat on Bonfire Night. A type of oatmeal gingerbread, it was very popular in Yorkshire because it was easy to access oatmeal. An early reference to Parkin can be found in 1728, when Anne Whittaker was accused of stealing oatmeal to make Parkin. Such was the popularity of the cake that the first Sunday in November was sometimes known as Parkin Sunday. In addition to Parkin, another favourite bonfire treat was Tom Trot, a type of homemade toffee. Recipes for Parkin and Tom Trot can be found on 7th and 14th November respectively.

The pranks played on Mischief Night on 4th November could often spill over onto Bonfire Night, as seen in this nineteenth-century report:

> In the days when there were no county police, if not wise enough to securely lock up your yard broom, of a certainty it would be stolen; and if ever you did see it again it would be in the evening of the fifth, soaked with tar, in the hands of some fellow rushing like a mad thing along the street with your property blazing in front of him. I have known scores of brooms which were stolen – aye, and stolen them myself – but I do not recollect an instance of the thief being prosecuted. No, if you did not secure your broom, it went, and that was very much the end of it. There was more fun running with a stolen broom than a bought one.

This was also a day for 'barring-out', in which children would lock the teacher outside the door until he promised them a holiday.

6th

The Model Botanic Guide to Health, published in Sheffield in 1893, claimed that 'Pennyroyal is a favourite herb for female derangement, removing all obstructions peculiar to women arising from obstructed perspirations'!

7th

There are many variations on the traditional Yorkshire Parkin cake – the 1917 *Yorkshire Cookery Book*, for example, lists seventeen different versions! This version, however, perhaps most closely resembles how it would have originally been made:

Ingredients

- 225g plain flour
- 225g medium oatmeal
- 113g brown sugar
- 1 level teaspoon ground ginger
- 113g butter
- 225g black treacle
- 1 egg
- ½ teaspoon bicarbonate of soda
- ¼ pint milk

Method

- Melt the sugar, butter and syrup over a low heat.
- Beat the egg and add to the syrup mix with some of the milk

- Sift the flour, oatmeal and ginger into a bowl and pour in the syrup mix
- Dissolve the bicarbonate of soda in the remaining milk and add to the rest of the mix
- Stir well, then transfer the mixture to a greased flat baking tin
- Bake until firm in a moderate oven for about an hour.
- Keep in a tin for a week before eating – it becomes deliciously stickier by the day!

8th

The village of Skinningrove, in 1535, reported the visit of a merman:

Old Men that would be loath to have their credyt crackt by a tale of a stale date, report confidently that sixty yeares since, or perhaps 80 or more, a sea-man was taken by the fishers of that place, where duringe many weeks they kepte in an oulde House, giving him rawe fishe to eate, for all other fare he refused; instead of voyce he shreaked, and hewed himself courteous to such as flocked farre and neare to visit him; – fayre maydes were wellcomest guests to his harbour, whome he woulde beholde with a very earneste countenaynce, as if his phlegmaticke breathe had been touched with a sparke of love. – One day, when the good demeanour of this new gueste had made his hosts secure of his abode with them, he prively stoale out of doores, and ere he coulde be overtaken recovered the Sea, whereinto he plounged himself; – yet as one that woulde not unmannerly depart without taking his leave, from the mydle upwardes he raysed his shoulders often above the waves, and making signs of acknowledgeing his good entertainment to such as beheld him on the shore, as they interpreted yt; – after a pretty while he dived downe and appeared no more.

9th

This early nineteenth-century broadside ballad, printed as 'The Bonny Grey' but known popularly as 'The Holbeck Moor Cockfight', has become a popular folksong. The original printed version, which dates from around 1833, described a battle between lads from Liverpool and Prescot, but upon entering Yorkshire it was changed to Holbeck and Oldham. Cock-fighting, a popular pastime among the working classes, was outlawed by Parliament in 1849. The following version is that of the one sung by the popular Yorkshire folkgroup, The Watersons.

>Come all of you cockers far and near,
>I'll tell you of a cock-fight, the when and where,
>On Holbeck Moor, as I've heard say,
>Between a black and a bonny grey.
>
>Twelve men from Hounslow Town they came,
>Along with them that brought their game;
>This game it was, as I've heard say,
>Of a black to fight with a bonny grey
>
>The first to come in were the Oldham lads;
>They come with all the money they had;
>The reason why, I heard them say,
>'The black's too big for the bonny grey.'
>
>Lord Derby he come swaggering down:
>'I'll lay two guineas to half a crown,
>Why, if the black he gets fair play,
>He'll have the wings off the bonny grey!'
>
>And when the clock struck one, two, three,
>The charcoal-black got pecked on the thigh;
>They picked him up to see fair play,
>But the black wouldn't fight with the bonny grey.

Cockfighting. Source: Wikimedia Commons

10th

Molly Cass was a witch from Leeming. One legend about her was that a man named George Winterfield refused to marry the girl he had made pregnant. A wrathful Molly appeared, as Eileen Rennison describes:

> She told him that the Devil had him and would never let him go. George was so frightened by her that he begged for a second chance and said that he would marry the girl. Molly declared that she seldom gave anyone a single chance let alone two. She told him 'the girl's waiting for thee George. She's asleep in the bulrushes. Go to her. All roads lead to the Swale tonight.' George hurried off immediately but he did not return that night. The next morning his body was found in the river and not far from that of his deserted sweetheart. She had drowned herself rather than face the shame of bearing an illegitimate child.

11th

It was believed that washing your hands in water which had been used to boil eggs could give you warts, and Rev. M. C. F. Morris recorded that an old lady informed him that she always threw away the water in which eggs had been boiled, for fear that it could be used for washing.

12th

Along the Doncaster bypass on the A1 can be found Robin Hood's Well. Originally built in 1710 near Skellow, it was moved in 1960 when construction of the motorway began. The name was given by Charles Howard, 3rd Earl of Carlisle – who built Castle Howard – in order to solidify the existing connections in folklore between Robin Hood and Barnsdale Forest. Nearby is a smaller well named after Little John.

Robin Hood's Well. Source: Wikimedia Commons

13th

Joe Castle, in Dulcie Lewis' collection of traditional Yorkshire cures, recalled his mother's tale of a holy healing well near Worrall, close to Sheffield. Called Owler Star, the water was used to treat everything from coughs and colds to fevers and stomach aches.

> Hot, sweating and having breathing problems, the sufferer lay upon a bed, probably just covered by a thin sheet, with bedroom windows wide open. [...] One of the children having been despatched a while ago with a bucket to collect some of Owler Star's water, returns and clomps up the wooden stairs, followed by the lady of the house. First, to detract attention from what was to happen, the patient was offered a glass of the water to drink, but warned to do so very slowly since the liquid was extremely cold. Meanwhile the remainder of the bucketful was poured into the clean washbowl. Into this was then placed a sponge or flannel to soak in the water. Having drunk their fill the patient put down the glass and enquired, 'What now?' Quickly, the covering sheet was removed and the sufferer exposed in nudity upon the bed. In a flash, the ice-cold cloth was – having been wrung out – swiftly brought down and pressed on the poor patient's tummy! The effect was immediate. So shocked was the sufferer that there was an instant leap from the bed and a rush downstairs, holding the midriff, followed by a call from upstairs. 'I knew that would cure you!'. Few, 'tis said, returned to their bed after a 'dose' – one way or another – of Owler Star's healing waters.

14th

Tom Trot toffee was a popular Yorkshire treat, especially on Guy Fawkes Night. Here is a recipe so you can make your own – although it does come with a considerable health warning!

Ingredients

- 125g butter
- 450g soft, brown sugar
- 60g black treacle
- 60g golden syrup
- 2 tbsp milk

Method

- Add all the ingredients to a medium-sized pan and bring to the boil, stirring continuously to prevent burning.
- Reduce to a simmer and cook for 15–20 minutes. To check whether it's ready, drop some of the mixture into a cup of cold water – if it goes brittle, it's ready.
- Pour the mixture into a well-greased tin and leave to cool completely.
- Once it's cooled and hardened, break into pieces with a heavy object. To prevent pieces of toffee from flying everywhere in the process, it's best to cover with cling film.

15th

Though foxhunting is controversial nowadays, it was once extremely popular in Yorkshire. J. Fairfax-Blakeborough, writing in 1956, recorded no less than twenty-one active packs of hunting hounds in the area. The Bilsdale Hunt, founded in 1668 by George Villiers, 2nd Duke of Buckingham, is reputed to be the oldest foxhunting pack in the country.

A foxhunting party at Burton Agnes, 1866. Source: Wikimedia Commons

16th

One unusual method of discovering the identity of a future lover was recorded in 1892. You must gather twelve sage-leaves at noon and put them into a saucer. They are to be kept there until midnight, at which point the window should be opened and one-by-one the sage-leaves dropped onto the street below with each chime of the clock. It was believed that the future husband would then be seen or heard in the street below.

17th

Today is one of four possible feast days of St Hilda, depending on the Christian denomination. A highly important figure in the early Christian church in England, she founded the abbeys at Whitby and Hackness, and local legend states that when seagulls fly over the abbey, they dip their wings in respect. In addition, she is said to have turned snakes into stone, and ammonite fossils – which look rather like petrified snakes – have been particularly associated with her. In fact, a genus of ammonite – *Hildoceras* – was named in her honour.

A carving of Saint Hilda, complete with seagulls and ammonite fossils. Source: Wikimedia Commons

18th

The study of folklore and customs often entails a significant amount of debate and uncertainty. Sometimes, when we see things in the past which we do not understand, we are tempted to reach wild conclusions as to their purpose. One such example is that of 'witch posts', which are St Andrew saltires carved into the wooden beams of houses. They are found almost exclusively in the North York Moors, and many folklorists believed that they were carved to protect the household from any witches who might come down the chimney. However, in recent years many have come to challenge this; witch posts are not mentioned by any of the leading Victorian folklorists, and there is little contemporary evidence to suggest that this was their purpose. Rather, it seems likely that the name 'witch posts' were given to these unexplained marks and the idea stuck.

19th

Wendy Milner, from Gargrave, recalled that an old lady – who had been taught this method from her grandmother – informed her that one way of stopping night cramps was to place a cork under your pillow.

20th

The village of Gilstead, near Bradford, was said to have a well which fairies could be seen drinking from. 'In olden times,' wrote Val Shepherd in her history of wells in Bradford, 'locals would visit it to drink the healing waters and leave rags called "memaws" tied to the trees as offerings.' There was also said to be a 'fairy hole' in a nearby rock. Fairy holes are small, natural holes which are too small to be explored by humans but were believed to house fairies.

21st

Foxhunting was once a very popular social activity which was woven into the fabric of upper-class society, as J. Fairfax-Blakeborough described in 1956:

> The York & Ainsty Hunt is an integral part of the tradition of the country just as are the St Leger, the Ebor, and the Gimcrack Stakes. The Hunt may not have the length of historical background of some of its neighbours, but there are a number of contributory factors which combine to make the York and Ainsty stand out as a cameo, wherever and whenever hunting in the great shire is mentioned. It has York, with its centuries of sporting tradition, as its centre. Almost from the outset it had quartered there famous cavalry regiments with distinguished sportsmen amongst the officers. Many generations of these, season by season, hunted with the York & Ainsty and carried away happy memories. [...] Then too, within the boundaries of the wide expanse of country are the homes of many of ancient lineage, most of them landowners, nearly all of them members of the Hunt.

European Fox. Source: Wikimedia Commons

22nd

It is not unusual, in Yorkshire, to find trees with hundreds of coins hammered or pushed into them. Known as 'wish trees', they have become popular tourist attractions. There are two famous wish trees in Yorkshire – at Bolton Abbey and the Ingleborough Nature Trail – as well as lesser-known ones, such as at Flintergill in Dent. It is also possible to find old wooden beams in houses which have coins pushed into them, such as The Old Hill Inn at Chapel-le-Dale.

A wish tree on the Ingleborough Nature Trail. Source: Wikimedia Commons

23rd*

In the days before official contracts between employer and employee were introduced, the most common way to get a job was to stand around in a 'hiring fair' and wait until a farmer, tradesman, or someone seeking domestic servants offered you a job for a year. The typical questions would be asked and, if the candidate was suitable, they would be given a verbal contract and a shilling to seal the deal. They would then be employed for that year up until the time of the next hiring fair, at which point they would be 'released' and free to seek another employer. Known as Martinmas Hiring Fairs, one unusual aspect is that, whilst St Martin's Day is on the 11th of November, fairs in Yorkshire often took place on or around the 23rd. This is because, when eleven days were cut from the calendar in 1752 as the country switched to the Gregorian calendar, Yorkshire kept the date of the Old Martinmas Day.

24th

St John's Well at Harpham was said to be able to calm wild animals. William of Malmesbury, writing in the eleventh century, wrote that it could tame the wildest of beasts, and that a rabid bull could become as gentle as a lamb before it.

25th

Rev. M. C. F. Morris recorded a dramatic encounter between a farmer and a witch. The farmer had lost a large number of cattle and, believing the witch to blame, began to beat her with a stick when he next saw her. Thinking that she still had him under her power, he resolved to ward her off with a well-known remedy. He filled in all the doors and holes of the building – to keep the witch out – then took the heart of an animal, stuck it with pins, and burnt it on the fire. The smell, it was believed, would then attract the witch to the house, where she would bark like a dog. Those in the house were not to speak or move, and then she would go away. The witch did, indeed, come to the house, yell, and go away, but the man himself died a few days later from wounds sustained in the fight with the witch. The man who had relayed the story to Morris genuinely believed that the witch had maintained great power over the farmer, despite his best efforts to the contrary.

26th

The origin of the place-name Halifax has given rise to two rather spurious legends. One is that the name derives from when a beautiful blonde woman spurned the advances of a lustful monk and had her head cut off as a result, the name 'hālig feax' (or 'holy hair') thus marking the place where her head was buried. The other is that the head of St John the Baptist was buried in the area after his execution. In reality, however, the name was recorded in the 1090s as 'Halyfax', likely deriving from the Old English 'halh-gefeaxe', meaning literally 'grassy corner'.

St. John the Baptist is featured on the gates of The Piece Hall in Halifax. Source: Wikimedia Commons

27th

At one time, as recorded in Leader's 1875 *Reminisces of Old Sheffield*, there was a legend in the city that Bonnie Prince Charlie, as he retreated to Scotland from Derby, stayed with a family in the city. They claimed that they were given a harpsichord, a wineglass, a sword, and other objects, but even Leader comments that there is no evidence to suggest that Bonnie Prince Charlie ever came to Sheffield.

28th*

The Sunday after the hiring fair was often the occasion for workers to be provided with a large meal before they left home to work. Called 'rive-kite Sunday', it literally means split-stomach Sunday – an indication of how much they would eat!

29th

Another place name of spurious origin is that of Everingham, in East Yorkshire. It was once thought to derive from St Everild, who founded a convent in the village in the seventh century. However, it is far likelier that the name derives from three Old English words, 'Eofer', meaning wild boar, 'ing', meaning people of, and 'ham', meaning settlement. This is similar to one of the early names for York, Eoforwic. This is because Everild is a rather minor saint of whom almost nothing is known, and so it is unlikely that an entire settlement would be named after her. In addition, no trace of the supposed convent at Everingham has been found, and its real location remains unknown.

30th*

There are many Dickens festivals in the country, but one of the most famous is the Grassington Dickens Festival, which is held in late November and early December each year. First held in the 1980s, it celebrates all things Dickensian, with re-enactments, costumes, talks, and fairs. Another popular festival is held at Malton, which boasts a considerable connection to Dickens: it is said that he was inspired to create the office of Bob Cratchit after visiting a close friend who lived there.

December

1st

This poem, 'The Funny Wedding', was published in *The Ballads and Songs of Yorkshire* in 1860 and describes a wedding 'which took place in Bradford on the First of December, 1851'.

>Just give attention, old and young,
>And listen for awhile,
>I'll sing to you a funny song,
>Will sure to make you smile,
>It is about a circumstance
>Well known to all around,
>I mean the funny wedding
>That took place in Bradford town.
>
>*Chorus.*
>
>Such a funny sight in Bradford town,
>Was never seen before.
>
>It was from Whipsey that the people
>On that morning came,
>The aged couple there did live,
>You perhaps may know their name;
>This couple long had wanted to
>Enjoy each other's bed,
>So on that happy day they went
>To Bradford to get wed.
>Such a funny wedding.
>
>They often told their tales of love,
>At length, good lack-a-day,
>Old Johnny said to Betty,
>'Love, this is our wedding day.'

Such mirth and fun in Bradford town,
The people did never see,
For John is sixty-five years old,
And Betty seventy-three.
Such a funny wedding.

Invitations were sent round to their
Neighbours and their friends,
And earnestly requested them
Their wedding to attend;
So on the first day of December,
They collected in their forces,
Some mounted upon donkeys' backs,
And others upon horses.
Such a funny wedding.

To see this funny wedding
Thousands gathered round,
For in a grand procession
They march'd into the town;
Some with soot mustachios,
Others with their faces black,
And another with a monkey
Stuft with straw upon his back.
Such a funny wedding.

There was some had got red jackets on,
And others had got blue,
With rummy caps and three-cock'd hats,
They seem'd a jovial crew,
And as they came along the street,
The people they did start,
And laugh to see old John and
Betty riding in a cart.
Such a funny wedding.

DECEMBER

At last they came up to the church,
And the cart did stand,
While John and Betty both got out,
As you shall understand;
He led her to the altar
And plac'd her by his side,
They took the oath, and Johnny then
Claim'd Betty for his bride.
Such a funny wedding.

When the marriage it was over,
Devoid of care or pain,
The procession got in readiness
For to return again.
With John and Betty in the cart
They made a grand display,
And as they homeward did return
The fifes and drums did play.
Such a funny wedding.

Now John and Betty have got wed,
Let's hope they will agree,
In unity and harmony
Always happy be,
And in nine months' time,
May they have a daughter or a son
Mark'd with this grand procession,
And December on its bum.
And such a funny wedding may
They live to see again.

2nd

Nappa Hall, in Wensleydale, has been the seat of the Metcalfe family for centuries, and there is a legend associated with the origin of their surname. One day, two men – named Wilfrid and Oswald – were walking in the dales when they suddenly saw a large, red animal in the distance. Wilfrid, thinking it was a lion, promptly ran away, but Oswald remained and saw that it was simply a red calf. From that day on, Oswald gained the surname Metcalfe and Wilfrid gained the name Lightfoot. This rather spurious story has many variations, and was perhaps used to poke fun at the origin of the Lightfoot surname. In reality, the name is likely of Anglo-Saxon origin.

3rd

Whitby fisherman, to soothe and heal their hands which were cracked with salt water and cold, would melt goose fat and mix it with gorse flowers to make a salve.

4th

Seeing a pantomime is a traditional part of Christmas for many families, but nobody mastered the art of theatre quite like the Victorians. Here are just a few of the performances offered in Leeds in 1866:

Ballet at the West Riding Concert Hall

A 'Gorgeous Christmas Revel' at Thornton's Music Hall and Theatre of Varieties

'Gonysetz's Spectroscope' at the Stock Exchange

'Grand Historical Equestrian scenes and Brilliant Spectacles' at Newsome's Grand Circus

'A Fairy Spectacular Entertainment on a scale of splendour never before attempted out of London, introducing a magnificent water scene entitled "The Titanic Cascades of Real Water and Sports of Fairy Land"', at Princess Concert Hall

Sadly, many of these theatres were later demolished, and one wonders whether the spectacular scenes which once graced the theatres of Leeds could be repeated today.

5th

Lilla Cross, which stands on Fylingdales moor, has become an iconic feature of the landscape. The legend associated with it holds that in the early seventh century King Edwin of Northumbria was travelling across the moors when an assassin – sent by the King of Wessex – suddenly leapt out in front of him. Lilla, Edwin's chief minister, jumped in front of the assassin and saved his life, but took the full force of the knife. He died, and the cross was erected in his memory. However, as nice as the story is, the cross likely dates from the tenth century – over three hundred years *after* the story is said to have taken place.

6th

On this day – the feast of St Nicholas, the patron saint of children – a 'boy bishop' was traditionally elected. Dressed in the clothes of the bishop and performing his ceremonies (except Mass), his authority would last until 28th December, the Feast of Holy Innocents. Though abolished by Elizabeth I, it has been revived in recent years across the country, including Ripon Cathedral.

7th

The ghost of Katherine Griffith, who died in 1620 at Burton Agnes Hall, was said to haunt the building. As the story goes, Anne had watched over the construction of the house and was determined to make it the most beautiful house ever built. When it was nearly finished, she went to visit the St Quintin family at Harpham (see 21st January), but near St John's Well she was attacked and robbed. She was brought back to Burton Agnes, but died a few days later of her injuries. Before she died, she told her sisters that she would never rest unless part of her could remain in the house. She made them promise that when she died, her head would be cut off and preserved in the Hall so she could keep watch over it. The sisters agreed – but only to pacify her – and when Anne died they buried her in the churchyard instead. The ghost of Anne began to haunt the Hall, and the sisters eventually agreed to exhume the body and remove the skull. It was brought into the house, and since then the Hall has not been haunted. Each time that the skull has been removed, however, the ghost has haunted the house. At some point it was built into the walls – though nobody knows for sure where – forever watching over the beautiful hall.

8th

Eileen Rennison, in her book *Yorkshire Witches*, recalled an unusual birth-related superstition:

> A caul is a thin membrane sometimes covering the face of a baby at birth. It was considered to be lucky; the child would never hang or drown and would have special powers that they could use for good or ill. Sailors would pay a good price for a caul as a safeguard against drowning, but mothers often kept it to give to the child when old enough. (As recently as the 1950s, when my son was born with a caul, the midwife asked me if I wanted to keep it).

9th

Henry Jenkins, of Bolton-on-Swale, is said to have lived to the ripe old age of 169. He claimed to have helped transport arrows to the battle of Flodden Field in Scotland in 1513 and worked as a fisherman on the River Swale for 140 years. Claiming a birth date of 1501, he died on this day in 1670, and is buried in St Mary's churchyard in Bolton-on-Swale.

A memorial to Henry Jenkins in Bolton-on-Swale, erected in 1743. Source: Catherine Warr

10th

A popular Yorkshire Christmas tradition is the performance of the choral masterpiece *Messiah*, by Handel. In 1768 the *Leeds Mercury* announced that it would be performed for eighteen nights throughout the winter, and since then there have been performances almost every year. In 1976, a thousand members of the public, together with a sixty-piece orchestra, sang *Messiah* for Radio Leeds. The public singing of *Messiah* has since become a tradition in its own right.

11th

A traditional Yorkshire Christmas treat is a Yule loaf. Often served with a glass of wine, it makes for a refreshing alternative to a heavy Christmas cake.

Ingredients

- 30g fresh yeast, or a sachet of dried
- ¼ pint tepid milk
- 225g butter
- 700g strong plain flour
- 3 eggs
- 225g each of currants and sultanas
- 225g sugar
- 85g mixed chopped orange peel
- 2 level teaspoons mixed spice or cinnamon

Method

- Dissolve yeast in the tepid milk, stir, and leave somewhere warm to foam for 15–25 minutes

- Rub the butter into the sifted flour, then add the sugar and spices
- When the yeast is ready add it to the mixture, then add the beaten eggs
- Cover the mixture and leave in a warm place for up to 2 hours to rise
- Punch it down, add the fruit and peel and mix well into the dough
- Put the dough into a lightly greased loaf tin. Cover with a damp tea towel and leave to rise again in a warm place for 15–25 minutes
- Cook in the centre of a moderate oven (180C/375F/gas mark 5) for 1 hour
- Glaze the top with melted honey or syrup.

12th

Calverley Old Hall is notorious for the terrible murders committed there in the seventeenth century, famously depicted in the 1608 play *A Yorkshire Tragedy*, which has been erroneously attributed to William Shakespeare. But what is interesting to us are the stories of ghosts which haunt the hall. Walter Calverley had, in 1604, murdered his two children before attempting to murder his wife, who only survived because the metal in her corset deflected his knife. He was caught whilst trying to escape and executed at York by being crushed between large stones.

After his execution it was said that his ghost could be seen galloping around the Calverley estate on a headless horse, accompanied by others and running down any unfortunates who happened to be in their way. These ghosts became so troublesome that the local vicar was driven to exorcising them, which seemed to work for a time – but they soon reappeared. A preacher in the eighteenth century, whilst staying at the Hall, recorded the following encounter:

I had not been asleep long before I thought something crept up to my breast, pressing me much. I was greatly agitated, and struggled hard to awake. In this situation, according to the best judgment I could form, the bed seemed to swing as if it had been slung in slings, and I was thrown out on the floor. When I came to myself I soon got on my knees, and returned thanks to God that I was not hurt. Committing myself to His care, I got into bed the second time. After lying for about fifteen minutes, reasoning with myself whether I had been thrown out of bed, or whether I had got out in my sleep, to satisfy me fully on this point, I was clearly thrown out a second time from between the bed-clothes to the floor, by just such a motion as before described. I quickly got on my knees to pray to the Almighty for my safety, and to thank Him that I was not hurt. After this I crept under the bed, to feel if there was anything there; but I found nothing. I got into bed for the third time. […] I had not lain a minute before I was thrown out of bed a third time.

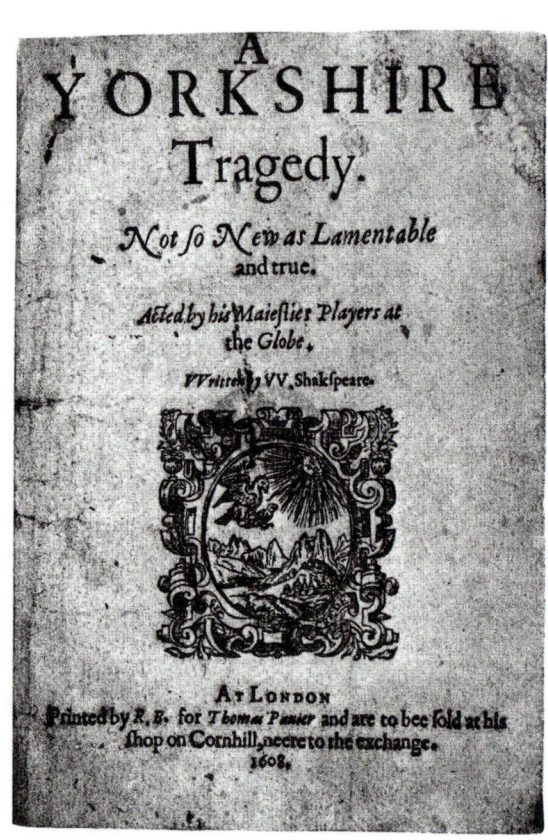

The play *A Yorkshire Tragedy* – originally assumed to be the work of Shakespeare, but now regarded as belonging to a different author – tells the story of the grim murders at Calverley Hall. Source: Wikimedia Commons

DECEMBER

13th

The guytrash, or padfoot, has an unusual association with water in Yorkshire folklore. Also known as 'Bloody Tongue', it was said to haunt a number of wells across Bradford and would either vanish or jump into the well if seen. As one witness recalled:

> When he [the guytrash] drank from the beck the water ran red right past the bridge down nearly to Bradford. As soon as it was dark he would lope up to the narrow flagged causeway to the cottage at the top of Bent Ing giving a deep bark … We used to sit [to look out for the dog] in the filled in pit which makes a hump in the middle of the field – only one girl saw him. A girl who lived at Headley had to go back home one night alone – her friends dare not go with her. They reached the end of the passage leading to the fields and gazed into the black well where Bloody Tongue resides but could go no further.

14th

A 'Barnsley chop' is a special type of lamb chop which is said to have first been served at a hotel in Barnsley in 1849. It was famously on the menu when the Prince of Wales – later Edward VIII – visited on this day in 1933. What makes it unique is the fact that it is a large, double loin chop which is rarely sold in supermarkets, and so if you want to experience it for yourself, you will have to find it at a local butcher's.

15th

'The tiny hamlet of Stone,' wrote Marie Hartley and Ella Pontefract in the 1940s, 'still had a curious custom connected with the eating of the Christmas dish of Frumenty. First the two eldest had to eat from the dish together, then the two next in age, down to the two youngest.'

16th

A figure called 'Peggy wi't Lantern' was also known to haunt wells around Bradford (see 13th December). A ghostly woman in a white night cap, she enticed unwary travellers to their doom with her lantern. She was said to wander to Jim Craven Well in Thornton, and it was known to avoid the area after nightfall.

17th

This rather bleak ballad, titled 'The Effects of Love' and printed throughout England in the nineteenth century, was said to derive from a true event. One of the earliest broadsides gave this as a background:

> Being a copy of verses found on the Humber Banks, near Hull. Enclosed in a letter to have been wrote by Miss W a young Lady of Hull, who drowned herself in the river Humber on Tuesday Night the 17th of December 1812 for the love of W. F. a shopkeeper by whom she was with Child, directed by her to be Published as a warning to all young Girls."

Whether the origin of the song as described is true or not is difficult to ascertain. The song itself is as follows:

> Young lovers all I pray draw near,
> Sad shocking news you soon shall hear,
> And when that you the same are told,
> It will make your very blood run cold,
> Miss B. W. is my name,
> I have brought myself to grief and shame,
> By loveing him that loves not me,
> With sorrow now I plainly see.

Mark well these words that will be said,
By W. F. I was betrayd,
By his false tongue I was beguil'd,
At length by him I was with child,
At rest with him I ne'er could be,
Until he had his will of me,
To his fond tales I did give way,
And did from paths of virtue stray.

My grief is more than I can bear,
I'm disregarded every where,
Like a blooming flower I am cut down,
And on me now my love does frown,
Of the false oathes he's sworn to me,
That I his lawful wife should be,
May I never prosper night nor day,
If I deceive you he would say.

But now the day is past and gone,
That he had fixed to be married on,
He scarcely speaks when we do meet,
And strives to shun me in the street,
I did propose on Sunday night,
To walk once more with my hearts delight.
On the Humber banks where billows roar,
We parted there to meet no more.

Since he is false a watery grave,
I have this night resolved to have,
I'll plunge myself into the deep,
And leave my friends behind to weep,
His word it was pledged to me,
He ne'r will prosper nor happy be,
My Ghost and my Infant dear,
Both shall haunt him every where.

Dear Dear William, when this you see,
Remember how you slighted me,
Farewell vain world, false man adieu,
I drown myself for love of you,
As a token that I died for love,
There will be seen a milk white dove,
Over my watery tomb will fly
There you will find my body lye.

These cheeks of mine once blooming red,
Must now be mingled with the dead,
From the deep waves to bed of clay,
Where I must sleep till judgment day,
A joyful riseing then I hope to have,
When angels call me from the grave,
Receive my soul Lord from on high,
For broken hearted I must die.

Grant me one favour that's all I crave,
Eight pretty maidens let me have,
Drest all in white, a comely show,
To take me to the grave bellow,
Now all young girls, I hope on earth,
Will be warned by my untimely death,
Take care sweet Maids when you are young,
Of Men deluding flattering tongue.

18th

One cautionary folk tale is that of Old Nanny of Lexhoe. One day, a farmer who lived near Stokesley was visited at midnight by the ghost of Old Nanny. She told him that under an apple tree in his orchard was a chest full of gold and silver, and that he was to dig it up and keep the silver for himself, but give the gold to a niece of hers who was impoverished. So off he went the next morning and, sure enough, there was a chest underneath an apple tree. However, instead of splitting the hoard as ordered, he decided to keep it all for himself. From that point on everything that could go wrong often did, and he became deeply unhappy. Every night the ghost of Old Nanny haunted him and followed him where he went. Eventually he was found dead on his own doorstep, a punishment for his disobedience.

Digging by an apple tree. Source: Vincent van Gogh, CC0, via Wikimedia Commons

19th

In the days before mechanised, large-scale transport, herds of geese would often be 'walked' from farms to markets to be sold. Marie Hartley and Joan Ingilby describe the method used:

> To prevent their webs from splitting [as they walked] they were driven through pens containing tar and sand, often at the blacksmith's shop. The rate of travel of a drove of 100–200 geese was half a mile an hour, and they had to be rested for half an hour each mile. Seven miles a day was good going, and allowing a fourteen-hour day, from 4 am to 6pm, it took six days to travel from Dent to Richmond [about 30 miles as the crow flies]. At Settle, where the geese were being driven down from the north, the men driving them wielded sticks with bladders tied at the end.

Starting off on this day, then, a goose farmer in Dent would be able to walk his herd to Richmond to be sold just in time for Christmas!

It was also common – especially in the Dales – to keep geese indoors, as they also describe:

> It was usual to house the sitting geese in the kitchen, perhaps under the table or in a corner with a few stones round and a little bedding, or in a tea box, or under the dairy shelves. Some cottagers might have as many as five or six sitting.

20th

Kirkham Priory, which sits on the banks of the River Derwent, was founded in the 1120s by Walter Espec, who also built Rievaulx Abbey. Legend has it that Kirkham was founded in memory of Walter's only son who had died nearby after being thrown from his horse when it was startled by a boar. The priory was dissolved in 1539, but later used to train troops and vehicles for the D-Day landings.

21st

Today is St Thomas' Day, and it was once customary to beg at the homes of farmers and the wealthier members of the community in order to obtain ingredients for frumenty. At Woodsome Hall, near Huddersfield, a sack of wheat stood at the door ready for everyone when they came 'a-Thomasin'. In Cleveland, children would carry an empty pillowcase into which farmers would give them a handful of corn. These practices of collecting grains were still being performed as late as 1909, but gradually were replaced by the collection of money and seasonal refreshments. At Barnes Hall, near Sheffield, widows who called would receive a glass of milk or ale, a slice of cake, and a sixpence.

Another tradition which takes place on this day is the Sheriff's Riding in York. The Sheriff, accompanied by musicians in full livery, process around the city. The musicians are The York Waits, a group which was at one time in existence for five hundred continual years before being abolished and later revived. Proclamations are made and horns blown at various points in the city, and the procession ends with the Sheriff's speech at the Mansion House. The proclamations welcome to the city 'whores, thieves, diceplayers and other unthrifty folk' for the twelve days of Yule.

The York Waits take part in the York Sherriff's Riding. Source: Averil Shepherd

22nd

Though difficult to find proof of the claim, William Strickland is said to have brought the first Turkeys to England. He seems to have gone a bit turkey mad; in 1550 his coat of arms included a turkey – alleged to be the oldest surviving European drawing of a turkey – and the parish church on his estate at Boynton is covered with turkeys. It even has a turkey lectern!

The turkey lectern at St. Andrew's Church, Boynton. Source: Wikimedia Commons

23rd

Thomas Kirkbride recalled a humorous tale of misunderstanding local customs:

> Our family lived in Askrigg [...] We were born in the Great War years, my sister Margaret and brother Sid; Shelagh came much later. Sid and I had been bathed one Friday night near Christmas time and when it was Margaret's turn we were ordered from the kitchen to the parlour to sit with Father. Suddenly we heard a scream from Mother and dashed through to the kitchen. There were four lads stood there, their faces smeared with black and they had just walked in without knocking. This was a local custom near Christmas and they had a little verse, 'Here comes I, nivver been afore, walked right in, wi'out knocking on the door!' They were lads who lived down the lane and their timing could not have been worse. Father grabbed his stick from the corner and chased them out!

24th

At the Minster Church of All Saints, in Dewsbury, a bell is tolled on Christmas Eve for every year since Jesus was born – making it ring over 2,000 times in recent years! Called 'The Devil's Knell', it heralds the death of the devil through the birth of Jesus. The custom is at least 600 years old, and local legend attributes the origin to the time when a local landowner in the fifteenth century murdered a servant and bought the church bell as penance.

Another popular custom was that of 'vessel cupping'. Believed to be a corruption of the word 'wassail', a small doll – representing the Virgin Mary – was placed in a box and decorated. One East Yorkshire woman recalled that small girls would go round neighbour's houses asking for a penny whilst carrying a box. If they were given a penny, the girls would then show them the doll inside the box.

DECEMBER

One unusual custom from Richmond is that of the Poor Old Hoss, or T'Owd 'Oss. Similar to the Welsh Mari Lwyd, it is a hobby horse – traditionally with a real horse skull on the top – accompanied by a group of mummers in huntsman costumes who beat it with sticks then revive it with a song and a blast on a hunting horn. They take T'Owd Hoss into pubs, shops, and any other public places unfortunate enough to be in their way!

Rev. M. C. F. Morris recorded a variety of Christmas Eve customs:

> On Christmas Eve the houses are decked with 'hollin' or other evergreens, which are never burnt afterwards, but thrown away. The Yule log used to be brought in and placed upon the fire along with a piece of that from the previous year which had been carefully preserved for good luck, in the same way as the Yuletide candle was. The Christmas candle is always a feature in the furnishing of the feast.

Minster Church of All Saints, Dewsbury. Source: Wikimedia Commons

It is lighted by the head of the house, and generally stands in the centre of the table, round which the members of the family sit to partake of the frumenty and other dainties that deck the board. No other candle must be lighted from it, and before the family retire to rest the master of the house blows it out, leaving what remains of it to stand where it is until the following morning. The unconsumed piece is then carefully stowed away with other similar relics of former years; sometimes quite a large number of such pieces are accumulated in the course of years: it is considered in some localities highly unlucky to disturb these remnants during the year. It was further thought unlucky not only, as I have said, to take a light from the Yule candle, but also to give a light to any one on Christmas Day; so that in former times, before matches were invented as we have them now, the question used to be asked before retiring to rest on Christmas Eve, 'is your tunder dhry?' In former times the Yule candle was looked upon as almost a sacred thing. If by any chance it went out, it was believed that some member of the family would die during the ensuing year, and if anyone in snuffing it extinguished the light, that person would, it was thought, die within the year.

The Poor Old Hoss, in Richmond. Source: Averil Shepherd

25th

In Whitby, as with New Year's Day, it was considered unlucky for fishermen to throw out the ashes or even to sweep up the dust on Christmas Day. It was also believed that oxen would kneel to honour the birth of Jesus; Rev. M. C. F. Morris recorded that it was common in Wensleydale for people to go out to the stable at midnight to see the oxen kneel.

According to one legend, St Paulinus of York (see October 10th) baptised ten thousand men and a multitude of women and children in the River Swale on this day in 627AD.

As you may have noticed throughout this book, Yorkshire people seem to have a bit of a thing for pies. Naturally, there was even a famous Yorkshire Christmas Pie. Often very elaborate, one recipe from 1796 calls for a turkey, goose, fowl, partridge, and a pigeon. 'Standing pies' were also common, often standing at nearly a foot high and filled with hare, rabbit, and pheasant. In Sheffield, in 1834, one pie was made which weighed almost 14 stone and contained 43 rabbits! By 1900, these pies had fallen out of fashion.

26th

Various types of sword dancing and mumming is popular on this day, as one 1811 gentleman's magazine describes:

> On the feast of St Stephen six youths (called sword dancers from their dancing with swords), clad in white and bedecked with ribbands, attended by a fiddler, and another youth curiously dressed, who generally has the name of Bessy, and also by one who impersonates a Doctor, begin to travel from village to village performing a ride dance called the sword dance. One of the six above-mentioned acts the part of a king in a kind of farce, which consists of singing and dancing, when the Bessy interferes, while they are making a hexagon with their swords, and is killed these frolicks they continue til New Year's

Day, when they spend their gains at the ale-house with the greatest innocence and mirth, having invited all their rustic acquaintance.

Similar to the Poor Owd Hoss (see December 24th), the Derby Tup is performed in Sheffield on Boxing Day. A mumming play, it involves a wooden ram's head on a pole, which is then carried round whilst the traditional folk song 'The Derby Ram' is sung.

Traditional sword dances are still performed on Boxing Day in Flamborough, and this dance has been described as one of the best in Yorkshire. There are also dances at Grenoside and Handsworth, as well as a competitive tug-of-war across the River Nidd in Knaresborough – all of which draw a significant number of spectators.

Boxing Day was also a popular time to go beagling, which saw its peak in the 1950s with the meet at the Devonshire Arms at Cracoe attracting crowds of almost five thousand people. Described as 'a rather complicated way of taking a walk', beagling is the hunting of hares on foot with a pack of hounds. As there is currently a ban on hare hunting, current beagling groups (such as the Airedale Beagles) hunt within the law and follow the legal limits and guidelines.

Sword dancing at Flamborough. Source: Wikimedia Commons

27th

Marie Hartley and Ella Pontefract, in their tour of the dales, recorded a rather unusual social activity:

> During the nineteenth century goose parties were a favourite form of entertainment in Snaizeholme. These were given in the week between Christmas and New Year's Day, and were attended only by the men. Whist was played all evening, and the man at whose house the party was held would give a goose as a prize, the winner of which invited them all back to his house the next night to play whist and eat the goose. He in his turn gave another goose for the prize, and the winner had to hold the party the next night, and so it went on until New Year's Day.

Domestic goose. Source: Wikimedia Commons

28th

This day, known as Childermas – or Holy Innocent's Day, as it remembers the time Herod ordered the death of all male infants in Bethlehem after the birth of Jesus – was known to be the unluckiest day of the year. No fisherman would set sail on this day, and nobody would seek to undertake important business either.

29th

The first ever competitive, knockout-style cup final in the history of Rugby was played on this day in 1877. Every single tournament in the Rugby Union and Rugby League world, from the World Cup to the Challenge Cup, can trace its origins to the final played at Leeds on Saturday 29th December 1877. A crowd of around two thousand spectators witnessed Halifax beat York for the RFU Yorkshire Cup, which is still running today. A long-running tradition in the Yorkshire sporting calendar, teams compete for 'T'Owd Tin Pot'.

30th

One popular odd character of Yorkshire folklore is Job Senior. He was once a strong, handsome young man who lived in and around Ilkley and Leeds, working variously as a labourer, dry-stone waller, oastler, and wool-comber. When he reached his sixties and was no longer able to work as he used to, he had the idea to set himself up for retirement. He met a widow named Mary, who lived in a cottage on Ilkley moor. Job thought that if he married the widow, the cottage and land would be his for life. He approached her – she was eighty years old – and with a bit of flattery, convinced her to marry him.

'It's an easy gotten penny by the light o' the moon,' he said to himself as he looked over his new domain.

Mary did not live long after that. As she was drawing close to death, Job drew her close to the fire and fried her some bacon. But she died as he was cooking it, and in shock he dropped the pan to the floor.

'Eh! But I musn't waste the fat,' he said. 'If t'ou'd lass cannot take it, why I mun eat it mysen.'

Unfortunately, the house and land did not pass to him upon her death, but rather to her family, and Job was inconsolable. The money he had hidden in the walls had been lost or stolen, the cottage was pulled down, and he spent the rest of his days living in a miserable hovel he'd made from the ruins of his house. 'His hut was like a dog-kennel; to enter it he was obliged to creep on hands and knees. Within it was only large enough for him to lie down in and turn himself about.' S. Baring-Gould describes his state:

> He used to walk leaning on two rough sticks, wearing a pair of heavy wooden clogs on his feet, stuffed with hay, his legs bandaged with straw. His coat was of many colours and much patched; his trousers were to match. He wore no braces, but kept his trousers in position with a hempen belt, part of an old horse-girth, which he buckled round his body. A bag on his back was fastened at the front to his belt. His head was adorned with a hat of the most antique shape, without a brim, and stitched together with hemp-string. The condition of his skin, which had not seen water for years, need not be described. His hair, once jetty black, now hung in heavy clotted locks on his shoulders. His eyebrows were back and prominent; his eyes low-set and watery. He wore a coarse beard, grizzled with age; and very dirty. From his hat depended a tobacco-pipe, hung by a string.

'Never,' he would say to visitors, 'never take to nowt, but whenever you can get a penny, felt [hide] it, and let nobody know about it, and then they cannot get it from you.'

It is believed that Job's end came after his drink was drugged as a prank at Silsden, and he caught cholera. He died at the age of seventy-seven, and was buried in Burley churchyard, near Otley.

31st

The 'Fragment of the Hagmena Song', as published in *The Ballads and Songs of Yorkshire* in 1860, was said to be sung in Richmond on New Year's Eve.

> To-night it is the New-year's night, to morrow is the day,
> And we are come for our right, and for our ray,
> As we used to do in old king Henry's day.
> Sing, fellows, sing, Hagman-heigh.
>
> If you go to the bacon-flick, cut me a good bit;
> Cut, cut and low, beware of your maw;
> Cut, cut and round, beware of your thumb,
> That me and my merry men may have some.
> Sing, fellows, sing, Hagman-heigh.
>
> If you go to the black-ark, bring me X mark;
> Ten mark, ten pound, throw it down upon the ground,
> That me and my merry men may have some.
> Sing, fellows, sing, Hagman-heigh.

Bibliography

Aubrey, J., *Miscellanies Upon Various Subjects*, www.gutenberg.org/ebooks/4254 (2003)
Baring-Gould, S., *Yorkshire Oddities, Incidents, and Strange Events Vol I*, fifth edition (Methuen and Co: London, 1900)
Baring-Gould, S., *Yorkshire Oddities, Incidents, and Strange Events Vol. II*, third edition (John Hodges: London, 1877)
Brears, P., *Traditional Food in Yorkshire* (John Donald Publishers Ltd: Edinburgh, 1987)
Clarke, D., *Supernatural Peak District* (Robert Hale: London, 2001)
Clarke, D., *Strange South Yorkshire: Myth, Magic and Memory in the Don Valley* (Sigma Leisure: Ammanford, 1994)
Crowther, A., *Yorkshire Customs: Traditions and Folklore of Old Yorkshire* (Dalesman Books: Lancaster, 1977)
Collard, G., *A Yorkshire Christmas* (Alan Sutton: Gloucester, 1989)
Cooper, Q. and P. Sullivan, *Maypoles, Martyrs & Mayhem* (Bloomsbury: London, 1994)
Davison Ingledew, C. J., *The Ballads and Songs of Yorkshire* (Bell and Daldy: London, 1860)
Deane, E., *Spadacrene Anglica, Or, The English Spa Fountain* (John Wright & Sons: London, 1922)
East Yorkshire Federation of Women's Institutes, *East Yorkshire: Within Living Memory* (Countryside Books: Newbury, 1998)
Farmer, David Hugh, *The Oxford Dictionary of Saints*, second edition (Oxford University Press: Oxford, 1987)
Fairfax-Blakeborough, J., *Foxhunting in Yorkshire* (Perivan Group Ltd: Southend-on-Sea, 1956)
Fitzgibbon, T., *A Taste of Yorkshire in Food and in Pictures* (Pan Books: London, 1979)
Forshaw, E. F., *Holroyd's Collection of Yorkshire Ballads* (George Bell & Sons: London, 1892)
Francis, J., *Chevin's Lee to Silver Hill* (Smith Settle Printing and Bookbinding Ltd: Otley, 2005)
Garla, D., 'The Day Sedbergh Grinds to a Halt', *The Dalesman* (March 1995)
Gee, H. L., *Folk Tales of Yorkshire* (Thomas Nelson and Sons Ltd: London, 1962)
Gill, A., 'Unlucky for Some in the Wolds Village', *The Dalesman* (October 1995)
Hartley, M. and J. Ingilby, *Life and Tradition in the Yorkshire Dales* (Dalesman: Keighley, 1981)
Hartley, M. and J. Ingilby, *Life and Tradition in West Yorkshire* (J. M. Dent & Sons Ltd: London, 1976)
Henderson, W., *Notes on the Folk-Lore of the Northern Counties of England and the Borders* (W. Satchell, Payton and Co: London, 1879)
Hope, R. C., *Holy Wells of England* (Elliot Stock: London, 1893)
Jeffrey, S., *Whitby Lore and Legend*, second edition (Horne & Son Ltd: Whitby, 1923)
Joy, D., *Life in the Yorkshire Coalfield* (Dalesman Books: Lancaster, 1989)
Jones, A. E., *Yorkshire Gypsy Fairs, Customs and Caravans 1885–1985* (Hutton Press: Bridlington, 1989)
Kellet, A., *The Yorkshire Dictionary of Dialect, Tradition and Folklore* (Smith Settle: Yeadon, 2007)
Leader, R. E., *Reminiscences of Old Sheffield, its Streets and its People* (Leader and Sons: Sheffield, 1875)
Lewis, D., *Down the Pan: A Nostalgic Look Back to the Good Old Days in North Yorkshire* (Countryside Books: Newbury, 2005)
Lewis, D., *Curious Cures of Old Yorkshire* (Countryside Books: Newbury, 2001)
Medcalf, A., 'Word play', *The Dalesman* (August 2020)
Moore, M. H., *A Yorkshire Cookbook* (David & Charles: London, 1980)
Morris, D., *The Swale: A History of the Holy River of St Paulinus* (William Sessions Limited: York, 1994)
Morris, Rev. M. C. F., *Yorkshire Folk-Talk* (Henry Frowde: London, 1892)

North Yorkshire Federation of Women's Institutes, *The North Yorkshire Village Book* (Countryside Books: Newbury, 1991)
Parkinson, T., *Yorkshire Legends and Traditions*, Vol I (Elliot Stock: London, 1888)
Parkinson, T., *Yorkshire Legends and Traditions*, Vol II (Elliot Stock: London, 1889)
Pontefract, E., and M. Hartley, *Wensleydale* (J. M. Dent & Sons Ltd: London, 1943)
Pontefract, E., and M. Hartley, *Swaledale* (J. M. Dent & Sons Ltd: London, 1946)
Pontefract, E., and M. Hartley, *Yorkshire Tour* (J. M. Dent and Sons Ltd: London,1946)
Rennison, E., *Yorkshire Witches* (Amberley Publishing: Gloucestershire, 2013)
Richardson, C., 'Beckball at Maltby', *The Dalesman* (June 1993)
Roud, S., *The English Year* (Penguin Books: London, 2006)
Mee, A., *Yorkshire: North Riding* (Hodder and Stoughton: London, 1960)
Mee, A., *Yorkshire: East Riding with York* (Hodder and Stoughton: London, 1964)
Mrs Simkins, 'Tom Trot toffee', *The Dalesman* (November 2017)
Shepherd, V., *Historic Wells In and Around Bradford* (Heart of Albion: Loughborough, 1994)
Short, Thomas, *Dr Short's History of Mineral Waters, &c* (F. Gyles: London, 1734)
Smith, J., 'Rushbearing Time', *The Dalesman* (August 1992)
Smith, J., 'Pace-Egging Time,' *The Dalesman* (April 1992)
Smith, J., 'Flamborough's Dazzling Day of Dance', *The Dalesman* (December 1993)
Smith, J., 'Anything goes at the Shrovetide Skip', *The Dalesman* (February 1994)
Taylor, Rev. R. V., *Anecdotae Eborancenses: Yorkshire Anecdotes or Remarkable Incidents in the Lives of Celebrated Yorkshire Men and Women* (Richard Jackson: Leeds, 1883)
Walker, G., *The Costume of Yorkshire* (T. Bensley: London, 1814)
Y. E. News, *You Don't Know Your Yorkshire!* (Y. E. News: Doncaster, 1952)

Useful Websites

airedalebeagles.com
barwickinelmethistoricalsociety.com
bedrace.co.uk
bridlington.net
bradfordmuseums.org
calendarcustoms.com
cricketyorkshire.com
denbydalepiehall.co.uk
dioceseofyork.org.uk
egtongooseberryshow.org.uk
foodsofengland.co.uk
fellponymuseum.org.uk
hardrawforce.com
hullfishingheritage.org.uk
insearchofholywellsandhealingsprings.com
leodis.net
lowercalderlegends.wordpress.com
middletononthewolds.co.uk
museumsintheyorkshiredales.co.uk

nationaltrust.org.uk
otleyshow.org.uk
oxenhopestrawrace.com
oxfordreference.com
pocklingtonhistory.com
richmond.org
rylstoneproject.com
ripon-internet.com
scarboroughsmaritimeheritage.org.uk
scortonarrow.com
slaithwaitemoonraking.org.uk
theakstons.co.uk
thegeorge-inn.co.uk
theyorkshiresociety.org
traditional-yorkshire-recipes.info
yorkshirefolksong.net
yorkshiregrub.co
whitbymuseum.org.uk

Websites attributed for images

Jan 4: https://digitalcollections.nypl.org/collections/the-costume-of-yorkshire-illustrated-by-a-series-of-forty-engravings-being#/?tab=about

Jan 11: https://digitalcollections.nypl.org/collections/the-costume-of-yorkshire-illustrated-by-a-series-of-forty-engravings-being#/?tab=about

Jan 16 https://www.shutterstock.com/image-vector/rn-plow-deep-plowing-j-cooke-342530720

Feb 1 https://digitalcollections.nypl.org/collections/the-costume-of-yorkshire-illustrated-by-a-series-of-forty-engravings-being#/?tab=about

Feb 3 https://digitalcollections.nypl.org/collections/the-costume-of-yorkshire-illustrated-by-a-series-of-forty-engravings-being#/?tab=about

Feb 5 https://www.shutterstock.com/image-photo/oat-plant-isolated-on-white-without-1846370515

Feb 6 https://digitalcollections.nypl.org/collections/the-costume-of-yorkshire-illustrated-by-a-series-of-forty-engravings-being#/?tab=about

Feb 9 https://commons.wikimedia.org/wiki/File:East_Window,_Holy_Trinity,_Micklegate,_York_(16103001204).jpg

Feb 10 https://wellcomecollection.org/works/vnnu68nq?wellcomeImagesUrl=/indexplus/image/V0007003.html

Feb 11 https://www.shutterstock.com/image-vector/hand-drawn-illustration-mill-eps-10-213808771

Feb 12 https://digitalcollections.nypl.org/collections/the-costume-of-yorkshire-illustrated-by-a-series-of-forty-engravings-being#/?tab=about

Feb 13 https://www.shutterstock.com/image-photo/adult-female-cow-resting-on-grass-381937666

Feb 24 https://commons.wikimedia.org/wiki/File:Cuckoo_(PSF).png

Mar 2 https://wellcomecollection.org/works/uwnxge8q

Mar 10 https://www.shutterstock.com/image-vector/loaf-bread-on-wooden-round-board-644344942

Mar 15 https://www.shutterstock.com/image-illustration/realistic-digital-color-scientific-illustration-haddock-1965478348

Mar 20 https://en.wikipedia.org/wiki/Gisborough_Priory#/media/File:Gisborough_priory_snow_portrait.jpg

Mar 22 https://www.shutterstock.com/image-vector/vector-illustration-engraving-big-hog-on-185923691

Mar 31 https://commons.wikimedia.org/wiki/File:Willy_Howe_Neolithic_round_barrow_(2)_(geograph_5741606).jpg

Apr 1 https://commons.wikimedia.org/wiki/File:Cottingley_fairies_illustration.jpg

Apr 6 https://www.shutterstock.com/image-vector/hand-drawn-sketch-yarn-ball-needles-533146405

Apr 7 https://www.geograph.org.uk/photo/6109658

Apr 17 https://www.alamy.com/stock-photo-goodall-backhouse-yorkshire-relish-1892-advert-for-the-celebrated-71148450.html?imageid=21C3E50F-8D5A-475C-9534-AF098FA9795B&p=28623&pn=1&searchId=3f0c18d7f5156868dd4257f0d9278309&searchtype=0

Apr 18 https://www.shutterstock.com/image-vector/cricket-ball-hitting-bowling-over-wicket-577942315

Apr 19 https://commons.wikimedia.org/wiki/File:Remains_of_John_o%27_Gaunt%27s_Castle.jpg

Apr 23 https://en.wikipedia.org/wiki/Saint_George_and_the_Dragon_(Raphael)#/media/File:Raphael_-_Saint_George_and_the_Dragon_-_Google_Art_Project.jpg

Apr 27 https://commons.wikimedia.org/wiki/File:Ingleborough,_north_face.jpg

Apr 30 https://commons.wikimedia.org/wiki/File:Dibbles_Bridge_-_geograph.org.uk_-_1757509.jpg

May 3 https://commons.wikimedia.org/wiki/File:Wade%27s_Causeway.jpg

May 10 https://commons.wikimedia.org/wiki/File:Rural_Sports_or_Game_at_Quoits_MET_DP881758.jpg

May 12 https://commons.wikimedia.org/wiki/File:Whitby_Penny_Hedge_Ceremony_(7216000682).jpg

May 19 https://www.shutterstock.com/image-photo/bee-boles-structure-set-garden-wall-1493156036

Jun 3 https://commons.wikimedia.org/wiki/File:Coventry-mystery-pageant-thomas-sharp-david-gee-1825.jpg

June 10 https://commons.wikimedia.org/wiki/File:Dry_stone_fences_in_the_Yorkshire_Dales,_England.jpg

Jun 20 https://commons.wikimedia.org/wiki/File:La_Main_de_Gloire.svg

Jun 23 https://digitalcollections.nypl.org/collections/the-costume-of-yorkshire-illustrated-by-a-series-of-forty-engravings-being#/?tab=about

Jul 1 https://commons.wikimedia.org/wiki/File:Image_taken_from_page_117_of_%27Spring-heel%27d_Jack_the_Terror_of_London._A_romance_of_the_nineteenth_century,_by_the_author_of_the_%E2%80%9CConfederate%27s_Daughter%E2%80%9D..._Illustrated,_etc%27_(11075681764).jpg

Jul 5 https://commons.wikimedia.org/wiki/File:Tom_Roberts_-_Shearing_the_rams_-_Google_Art_Project.jpg
Jul 9 https://www.shutterstock.com/image-vector/ass-vintage-engraved-illustration-dictionary-words-331644200
Jul 11 https://commons.wikimedia.org/wiki/File:James_Clarke_Hook_-_Boys_Collecting_Eggs_on_Cliff_Face_-_B1977.14.11754_-_Yale_Center_for_British_Art.jpg
Jul 13 https://commons.wikimedia.org/wiki/File:Cleveland_Way_at_Live_Moor.jpg
Jul 18 https://commons.wikimedia.org/wiki/File:Gypsy_caravan.jpg
Jul 29 https://beverleyminster.org.uk/
Aug 20 https://www.shutterstock.com/image-vector/moon-crescents-set-drawings-engraving-style-2048778392
Aug 23 https://en.wikipedia.org/wiki/Swing_boat#/media/File:Carter's_Steam_Fair,_Prospect_Park_-_geograph.org.uk_-_1002180.jpg
Aug 24 https://commons.wikimedia.org/wiki/File:Rush_Bearing_at_Long_Millgate,_Manchester.jpg
Aug 25 https://commons.wikimedia.org/wiki/File:LeedsCarnival20085571.jpg
Sep 6 https://commons.wikimedia.org/wiki/File:The_Rushcart_(28881965954).jpg
Sep 8 https://en.wikipedia.org/wiki/Hardraw_Force#/media/File:Hardraw_Force_Jan_22.jpg
Sep 10 https://www.shutterstock.com/image-vector/hand-drawn-rowan-branch-vintage-style-1845428359
Sep 11 https://commons.wikimedia.org/wiki/File:Lampe_-_The_Dragon_of_Wantley_-_Moore_fighting_with_ye_Dragon.png
Sep 13 https://commons.wikimedia.org/wiki/File:Robin_Hood_and_Guy_of_Gisborne.jpg
Sep 14 https://commons.wikimedia.org/wiki/File:John_Harris_Jr._-_Doncaster_Races,_Race_for_the_Great_St._Leger_Stakes,_1836_-_Joy_%5E_Desperation%5E_Allover_but_Settling_-_B1985.36.824_-_Yale_Center_for_British_Art.jpg
Sep 16 https://wellcomecollection.org/works/xdatycm4
Sep 23 https://commons.wikimedia.org/wiki/File:The_Nidderdale_Show_is_held_annually_on_the_showground_by_the_River_Nidd._-_panoramio.jpg
Oct 10 https://wellcomecollection.org/works/m7th44zs
Oct 11 https://commons.wikimedia.org/wiki/File:Hull_Fair,_Giant_Wheel_-_panoramio.jpg
Oct 15 https://commons.wikimedia.org/wiki/File:Barnsley,_Cheapside.jpg
Oct 16 https://commons.wikimedia.org/wiki/File:Castleton,_North_Yorkshire.jpg
Oct 21 https://en.wikipedia.org/wiki/John_Twenge#/media/File:British_Library_Royal_17_B_XLIII_St_John_of_Bridlington_in_St_Patricks_Purgatory.jpg
Oct 28 https://en.wikipedia.org/wiki/Simon_the_Zealot#/media/File:Rubens_apostel_simon.jpg
Oct 30 https://upload.wikimedia.org/wikipedia/commons/1/10/Diskharrow.png
Nov 2 https://commons.wikimedia.org/wiki/File:Soul_cakes.jpg
Nov 9 https://en.wikipedia.org/wiki/Cockfight#/media/File:Microcosm_of_London_Plate_018_-_Royal_Cock_Pit_(colour).jpg
Nov 12 https://commons.wikimedia.org/wiki/File:Robin_Hood%27s_Well.jpg
Nov 15 https://commons.wikimedia.org/wiki/File:CS_pl.094_-_Burton_Constable,_Yorkshire_-_Morris%27s_County_Seats,_1867.jpg
Nov 17 https://commons.wikimedia.org/wiki/File:St_Hilda_memorial_ammonites.jpg
Nov 21 https://commons.wikimedia.org/wiki/File:Fox_-_British_Wildlife_Centre_(17429406401).jpg
Nov 22 https://commons.wikimedia.org/wiki/File:Wish_Tree_on_a_yew,_Ingleborough_Nature_Trail,_Clapham,_Yorkshire.jpg
Nov 26 https://commons.wikimedia.org/wiki/File:Piece_Hall_Gates_(13497384015).jpg
Dec 12 https://commons.wikimedia.org/wiki/File:Yorkshire_Tragedy_1608_TP.jpg
Dec 22 https://commons.wikimedia.org/wiki/File:Boynton,_St_Andrew%27s_church,_turkey_lectern_(27946814237).jpg
Dec 24 https://en.wikipedia.org/wiki/Dewsbury_Minster#/media/File:Dewsbury_Minster_in_2021.jpg
Dec 26 https://commons.wikimedia.org/wiki/File:Flamborough_Sword_Dance_Boxing_Day_2010_-_2_-_geograph.org.uk_-_2215104.jpg
Dec 27 https://en.wikipedia.org/wiki/Domestic_goose#/media/File:Domestic_Goose.jpg

Index

Customs

Antient Silver Arrow Contest, May 18
Awd Roy, Jan 6
Barring-out, Feb 16, Nov 5
Beagling, Dec 26
Bear-Baiting, June 29
Bed Race, June 8
Blessing of the Boats, June 13
Bloody Thursday, Feb 18
Boy Bishop, Dec 6
Broughton Hall Game Show, June 26
Burials, March 9, Sep 28
Burning of the Bartle, August 24
Carling Sunday, March 14
Chalking, May 16
Coal Carrying, April 5
Collop Monday, Feb 15
Corpus Christi, June 3
Court Leet, Oct 3
Coxwold Sunday, May 12
Cricket, April 18, August 26
Devil's Knell, Dec 24
Dickens Festival, Nov 30
Divination, Jan 2, Feb 14, April 4, June 5, July 30, Oct 31, Nov 16
Dumb Cake, Jan 20, June 23
Feasts;
  Bellerby, May 31
  Hepworth, June 24
  Kilburn, July 7, July 12
  Middleton, June 11
  Redmire, Sep 21
Dry stone walling, June 10
Egg collecting, July 11
Fellsman Hike, April 21
Fig Sunday, March 28
Fire Festival, Feb 2
First-footing, Jan 1
Friendly Societies, Coverdale, June 9
Foxhunting, Nov 15, Nov 21
Hash Wednesday, Feb 17
Havercake Lads, Feb 1
Hay Ride, June 17
Hiring fair, Nov 23
Horn-blowing, Jan 22, Oct 1
Kissing Friday, Feb 19
Kiplingcotes Derby, March 18
Knurr-and-Spell, Feb 6
Lent, March 1
Liquorice Festival, July 7
Longsword dancing, Jan 10, Jan 16, Dec 26
Lost Trawlermen's day, Jan 26
Lyke Wake Walk, July 13
Maundy Thursday, April 15
May Day, May 1, May 4
Maypoles, April 5
May Stir, May 14
Mell Supper, Sep 15
Messiah [Handel], Dec 10
Midsummer Eve, June 23
Mischief Night, Oct 31, Nov 4, Nov 5
Mumming, Jan 11, April 2, Sep 15, Dec 26
Moonraking festival, Feb 20
Mystery Plays, June 3
Nippsy, May 8
Oak Apple day, May 29
Pace eggs, April 2, April 4
Parkin Sunday, Nov 5
Penny Hedge, May 12
Penny-scrambling, Jan 1
Pies, June 15, August 1, August 27, August 28, August 29, Sept 3, Sept 5, Dec 25
Plough Sunday, Jan 10, Jan 16
Plough Monday, Jan 11
Poor Old Hoss, Dec 24
Richmond Meet, May 27
Riding the Stang, Jan 4
Rive-kite Sunday, Nov 28
Rugby League, April 24, Dec 29
Shows and fairs,
  Boroughbridge, June 11
  Bowling, May 23
  Great Yorkshire Show, July 14
  Halifax, August 23
  Hull, Oct 11
  Lee Gap, August 13
  Nidderdale, 23 Sep
  Otley, May 18,
  Scarborough, August 15

278

Seamer, July 15
Topcliffe, July 18
West Indian Carnival, August 25
Wibsey, Oct 9
Yarm, Oct 17
Rush Week *see Wakes Week*
Rushbearing, August 21, August 24, Sept 6
Septennial Boundary Riding, August 29
Sheep dog trials, June 22
Sherriff's Riding, Dec 21
Shrovetide skipping, Feb 16
Souling, Nov 2
Spaw Sunday, May 2
Spells, Oct 26
Straw Race, July 7
Three Peaks Race, April 27
Thump Sunday, June 27
Topcliffe, March 25
Trinity Sunday, May 30
Trussing in, Oct 7
Quoits, May 10, Sep 21
Vardy Dinner, July 3
Vessel cupping, Dec 24
Wakes Week, June 28
Wallops, Jan 25, Sep 21
Weddings, March 7, May 20, May 25, July 10, July 17, July 21, July 27, July 29, August 4, August 7
Well dressing, May 21
White Hats and Black Hats match, May 2
Whitmonday, May 23
Whit Walk, July 31
Wilson Run, March 26
Yan-Tan-Tethera, April 6

Folklore

Austwick, Feb 21, Feb 22, Feb 23, Feb 24
Baptism, August 31, Sep 29
Barghest, Feb 28, Oct 27, Dec 13
Bees, May 19, July 22
Beggar's Bridge, *see Lover's Bridge*
Birth, August 14
Boy of Egremont, Feb 27
Bradford Boar, March 11
Brother Jucundus, March 30
Caedmon, April 28
Christopher Pivett, March 4
Churn supper, Sep 1
Devil, Feb 7, March 15, April 25, April 30
Dragons, Jan 28, May 17, July 8
Drummer Boy of Richmond, April 20
Fairies, March 24, March 31, April 1, April 7, April 8, April 26, June 14, Oct 13, Nov 20, Nov 18
Giants, Feb 11, May 3
Ghosts, Jan 5, Feb 9, April 14, July 1, July 28, August 8, August 9, Sep 2, Sep 10, Dec 7, Dec 12, Dec 16
Guytrash, *see Barghest*
Hand of Glory, June 20
Hazel, April 2, April 3, August 22
Haverah Park, April 19
Henry Jenkins, Dec 9
Hobmen, Feb 25, Sep 20
Hole of Horcum, April 22
Hollow Mill Cross, Sep 12
Jenny Greenteeth, June 16
Job Senior, Dec 30
Lilla's Cross, Dec 5
Lost Town of Semerwater, Jan 31
Lover's Bridge, Jan 24
Mermen, Nov 8
Metcalfe, Dec 2
Mother Shipton, Sep 16
Old Boots, Jan 5
Old John Mealy Face, March 25
Old Nanny of Lexhoe, Dec 18
Padfoot, *see Barghest*
Penhill Giant, Feb 4
Potter Thompson, Oct 14
Robin Hood, July 20, August 5, Sep 13, Sep 18, Nov 12
Sir Percival Cresacre, Jan 7
Spring-Heeled Jack, July 1
St Leonard's Cross, March 6
Stone heads, March 16
Superstitions,
  Birth, Dec 8, April 11, July 26
  Cats, Oct 23
  Death, July 23, Sep 7
  Farming, Feb 29, April 3
  Fishing, Jan 1, Feb 2, Dec 25, Dec 28
Three Laps, Jan 19
Upsall Gold, Oct 29
Vampire, Jan 13
Wish trees, Nov 22
Wells,
  Black Tom's, March 27

Drumming, Jan 21
Ebbing and Flowing, Jan 14
Gilstead, Nov 20
Holy Lady Healing, August 2
Old Wives' Well, July 16
Owler Star, Nov 13
Pin, June 7, June 14
Rag, Jan 27
St Antony's, Oct 4
St John's. Nov 24
Valley Parade, March 13
Zouche, July 4
Whitby Abbey Bells, March 12
White Doe of Rylstone, Jan 3
Willance's Leap, Nov 3
Witches, Jan 17, March 8, April 13, July 6, July 24, Aug 16, Sep 26, Oct 2, Sep 9, Oct 5, Oct 6, Nov 10, Nov 25, Oct 19

Places

Askrigg, Dec 23
Austwick, Feb 21, Feb 22, Feb 23, Feb 24
Bainbridge, Oct 1
Barnburgh, Jan 7
Barnsdale, Sep 13, Nov 12
Barnsley, Oct 15, Dec 14
Barwick-in-Elmet, April 5, May 1
Bedale, Jan 9, April 9
Bellerby, May 31
Bempton, July 11
Beverley, April 4, May 5, May 7, May 9, June 29
Bilsdale, Nov 15

Bingley, Oct 4
Bolton Abbey, Jan 3, Nov 22
Bolton-on-Swale, Dec 9
Boroughbridge, Feb 7
Bowland, July 5
Boynton, Dec 22
Bradford, Feb 3, Dec 1, March 11, March 13, May 23, June 21, July 31, August 9, Oct 9, Dec 13, Dec 16
Brayton, June 14
Bridlington, May 16, Oct 21
Brighouse, June 28, August 21
Broughton Hall, June 26
Burnsall, May 1, August 24
Burton Agnes, Dec 7
Calverley Hall, Dec 12
Castle Bolton, May 24
Castleford, March 3
Castleton, Oct 16
Cawood, April 14
Chapel-le-Dale, Nov 22
Cleckheaton, March 19
Copgrove, April 10
Cottingley, April 1
Coverham, Oct 28
Coxwold, May 12
Cracoe, Dec 26
Crayke, May 5
Dalton, Sep 29
Danby, Oct 5
Denby Dale, June 15, August 1, August 27, August 28, August 29, Sept 3, Sept 5
Dent, Jan 13, Feb 12, Nov 22

Dewsbury, Dec 24
Doncaster, Sep 14
Driffield, Jan 1
Easby, Oct 2
Egton, August 6
Everingham, Nov 29
Faceby, March 10
Farndale, Feb 25
Filey, March 15
Flamborough, July 11, Dec 26
Fylingdales, Dec 5
Gamsworth, May 19
Gargrave, Nov 19
Gawthorpe, April 5, May 4
Giggleswick, Jan 14, March 28
Gilstead, Nov 20
Guisborough, Jan 4, March 20
Grassington, April 7, June 25, Nov 30
Great Ayton, Oct 2
Halifax, Jan 17, June 27, August 23, Nov 26, Dec 29
Harden, Oct 4
Harden Moss, June 22
Hardraw Force, Sep 8
Harrogate, March 2
Harpham, Jan 21, May 5, May 9, Nov 24
Haworth, March 16, Oct 27
Helmsley, July 3
Hepworth, June 24
Hubberholme, Jan 6
Huddersfield, August 28, Oct 12, Dec 21
Hull, Jan 26, Dec 17, Oct 11
Ilkley, April 8, May 2, Dec 30

Ingleborough, Nov 22
Keld, May 14, June 2
Kilburn, July 7, July 12, Sep 15
Kiplingcotes, March 18
Kirby Hill, August 29
Kirkby Lonsdale, April 25
Kirkbymoorside, April 13
Kirkham Priory, Dec 20
Knaresborough, April 15, April 19, June 8, Sep 16, Sep 24, Dec 26
Knottingley, June 9
Laycock, Jan 19
Leeds, April 24, August 7, Nov 9, August 13, August 19, August 25, Oct 25, Nov 12, Dec 4, Dec 10, Dec 29, Dec 30
Leeming, Nov 10
Leyburn, Oct 6
Lexhoe, Dec 18
Lightcliffe, August 21
Lockwood, Sep 30
Maltby, June 1
Malton, Nov 30
Market Weighton, Feb 10
Marsden, Feb 2
Masham, Jan 18, Oct 7
Muker, Jan 6
Nappa Hall, Dec 2
Newburgh Priory, June 21
Newton Kyme, March 27
Nunnington, May 17
Otley, May 18
Oxenhope, July 7
Pately Bridge, Sep 23
Penistone, May 21
Pontefract, Feb 8, July 7
Rastrick, August 21
Redmire, Sep 21

Richmond, April 20, May 27, August 29, Oct 14, Nov 3, Dec 24
Ripon, Jan 1, Jan 5, Jan 22, August 3, Dec 6
Rotherham, May 8, Sep 17
Runswick Bay, Sep 20
Saddleworth, August 24
Scarborough, Feb 16, August 15, August 26
Scorton, May 18
Sessay, Feb 11
Settle, August 19
Sexhow, July 8
Sheffield, July 19, Feb 13, April 16, July 1, August 8, Sep 2, Nov 6, Nov 27, Dec 21, Dec 25, Dec 26
Skinningrove, Nov 8
Slaithwaite, Feb 20
Slingsby, Jan 28
Snaizeholme, Dec 27
Sneaton, Jan 12
Sowerby Bridge, Sep 6
Spaunton, Oct 3
Stape, July 16
Stamford Bridge, Sep 25
Stone, Dec 15
Thorne, August 31
Thorpe, April 30
Threshfield, August 2
Thrybergh, March 6
Thwing, Oct 21
Topcliffe, July 18
Upsall, Oct 29
Wakefield, Aug 18, March 17, July 20, Oct 26
Walkington, June 17
Walton, Jan 27
Wantley, Sep 11
Westerdale, July 23

West Witton, August 24
Whitby, Jan 12, March 12, March 29, April 2, April 4, April 28, May 7, May 12, May 30, June 13, June 20, July 21, August 10, August 17, Sep 27, Oct 13, Oct 29, Oct 31, Nov 17, Dec 3, Dec 25
Willy Howe, March 31
Worrall, Nov 13
Yarm, April 3, July 25, Oct 17
York, Jan 12, March 4, March 8, March 22, April 23, June 3, July 4, July 28, August 30, Sep 24, Sep 10, Oct 18, Nov 21, Dec 21, Dec 29

Recipes

Cheesecakes *see Curd tarts*
Curd tarts, March 21
Dock Pudding, June 6
Dumb Cake, Jan 30
Frumenty, Jan 23
Fruttaces, Feb 26
Harrogate tart, May 22
Oatcakes, Feb 5
Parkin, Nov 7
Pepper-cake, May 11
Tom trot toffee, Nov 14
York Mayne Bread, April 12
Yorkshire Get-Well Cake, Sep 22
Yorkshire relish, April 17
Yule loaf, Dec 11

Remedies

Jan 9, Jan 29, Feb 13, March 2, March 5, March 19, April 8, April 9, April 10, April 16, May 13, May 24, May 28, June 12, July 9, July 25, August 20, Sep 27, Sep 30, Oct 8, Oct 12, Oct 20, Oct 30, Nov 6, Nov 13, Nov 19, Dec 3

Saints

Alkelda, March 28
Antony, Oct 4
Barnaby, June 11
Bartholomew, August 24
Begu, Oct 31
Blaise, Feb 3
Ecca, May 5
Everild, Nov 29
George, April 23
Hilda, Oct 31, Nov 17
John the Baptist, June 27, Nov 26
John of Beverley, May 5, May 7, May 9, Nov 24
John of Bridlington, Oct 21
Leger, Sep 14
Luke, Oct 18
Margaret Clitherow, August 30
Mark, April 24
Nicholas, Dec 6
Paulinus, Oct 10, Dec 25
Robert of Knaresborough, Sep 24
Simon the Zealot, Oct 28
Thomas, Dec 21
Wilfrid, August 3
William of York, June 8

Songs and poems

Barnsley Anthem, Oct 15
Craven Churn-Supper Song, Sep 4
Dragon of Wantley, Sep 11
Effects of Love, Dec 17
Fragment of the Hagmena Song, Dec 31
Funny Wedding, Dec 1
Heckler Lad, Mar 17
Holbeck Moor Cockfight, Nov 9
Kilburn Feast song, July 12
Lyke Wake Dirge, June 4
Old Woman in Yorkshire, Jan 8
Pit Boy, June 19
Pony Driver's Song, March 3
Richmond Cricketers, April 18
Rothwell Debtors' Prison Song, Aug 18
Sheffield Park, July 19
Wensleydale lad, Jan 15
Yorkshire Bite, May 26
Yorkshire Motto, Aug 11

About the Author

Catherine Warr was born in Leeds in 1999 and graduated from the University of Bradford in 2020 with a degree in Peace Studies. Her YouTube channel, 'Yorkshire's Hidden History', has amassed thousands of views from all over the world and she has quickly established herself as an eminent young, local historian. In 2021 she joined the British Association for Local History as Engagement Fellow and her work has been featured in a national YouTube campaign.